THE ARMIES OF BACTRIA
700 BC - 450 AD

VOLUME 2 (ILLUSTRATIONS)

Valerii P Nikonorov

Colour Plates by Rory Little

Black & White Art by Alexander Sil'nov

Published by Montvert Publications

Published in 1997 by Montvert Publications

© Copyright Montvert Publications

Montvert Publications, 2 Kingswood Grove, Reddish, Stockport SK5 6SP

Montvert (Distribution), PO Box 25, Stockport SK5 6RU

ISBN 1-874101-10-8 (set)

A CIP catalogue record for this book is available from the British Library.

Typeset by MONTSET, Stockport, Cheshire

Printed by Joseph Ward Colourprint, Yorkshire, UK

CONTENTS (VOLUME 2)

FIGURE CAPTIONS

COLOUR PLATE DESCRIPTIONS

COLOUR PLATES

FIGURES

Note: This is Volume 2 of a two-volume set. For main text see Volume 1.

A note to the reader: This is one of a series of Montvert titles which aim to present some of the best up-to-date analyses of the history, dress, equipment and organization of various ancient and medieval armies.

Dr Philip Greenough (Editor)

FRONTISPIECE - Nomadic Conquerors and Lords of Bactria
(1st century BC to mid-1st century AD).

(LEFT)   Indo-Saca/Scythian ruler Spalirises (first quarter of 1st century BC)
(RIGHT) Early Kushan sovereign of Bactria   (about mid-1st century AD)

(See Page 24 for full description)

FIGURE CAPTIONS

Figure 1: (a-d) Bronze bilobate arrowheads of the Late Bronze Age (early 1st millennium BC) from Southern Bactria - (a) socketed one from the Dashly oasis and (b-d) tanged ones from Dil'berjin and Tillya-tepe (after Yagodin V N in *Drevnyaya Baktriya 3*, ed by I T Kruglikova. Moskva, 1984, Fig 2). (e-j) Bronze bilobate arrowheads from Kutlug-tepe (Southern Bactria), 8th to mid-6th century BC. (e-h) socketed and (i, j) tanged. (k-n) Bronze trilobate and socketed arrowheads from Altyn-10 (Southern Bactria), the second half of 6th-5th century BC (also after Yagodin V N, *op cit*, Fig 1). (o-cc) Bronze arrowheads from Takht-i Sangin, 5th-4th century BC - (o) bilobate and socketed, (p-bb) trilobate and socketed, (cc) trilobate and tanged (after Litvinskii B A in *Drevnosti Evrazii v skifo-sarmatskoe vremya*, ed by A I Melyukova and others. Moskva, 1984, p.155). (dd) Silver disc, partially gilt, ornamented with relievo scenes of hunting, in which three riders (see Fig 3a-c) pursue game; it belongs to the Oxus Treasure collection (cat no 24) and is dated 5th-4th century BC; such a disc must have been used as either a shield boss (*umbo*) or a horse's *phalera* (drawing after Dalton O M, 1905).

Figure 2: (a) Relief of the Apadana built by Darius I (522-486 BC) at Persepolis, showing one of the 23 tributary delegations of the king's subject nations, namely Delegation No. XIII which should be identified with the Bactrians (see Schmidt E F, 1970, p.148). (b) Detail of this relief - a Bactrian no. 3 with two bowls (drawings after Walser G, 1966, Pls. 20 and 62). (c, d) Bactrian throne-bearers (nos. 6) on reliefs of the Persepolis royal tombs - (c) Tomb II, of Xerxes (486-465) and (d) Tomb VI, of Artaxerxes III (359-338) (drawings after Schmidt E F, 1970, Fig 41). (e) Bactrian leading a camel, depicted on a gold plaque from the Oxus Temple at Takht-i Sangin, 5th cent. BC (drawing after Pichikyan I R, 1991, ill. 13). (f) Bactrian throne-bearer on a stone relief in the Hall of 100 Columns at Persepolis (after Walser G, 1996, p 62).

Figure 3: (a-c) Hunters from the silver disc of the Oxus Treasure (cat no 24); see our Fig. 1dd as well as Pl 1C as their summarised reconstruction (drawings after Dalton O M, 1905). (d) Lightly armed mounted lancer represented on a terracotta flask fragment found at Koi-Krylgan-kala in Khorezmia, 4th - early 3rd century BC (after Vorob'iova M G in *Koi-Krylgan-kala - pamyatnik kul'tury drevnego Khorezma IV v. do n e - IV v n e*, ed by S P Tolstov and B I Vainberg. Moskva, 1967, p.203, Fig. 27,6).

Figure 4: (a) Priest wearing "Median" dress, depicted on a gold plaque from the Oxus Treasure (cat no 48), 5th-4th century BC; see for detail on his equipment Pl 1A. (b) Spearman in "Median" dress on a gold plaque of the same date also from the Oxus Treasure (cat no 73); see Pl 1B. (c) Another gold plaque from the same collection (cat no 84), with an armoured warrior's representation, 4th century BC; see Pl 1D. (d) Three views of a rider's figurine of gold, who is dressed in a tall headgear, short tunic and tight trousers; from the Oxus Treasure (cat no 7b), 5th-4th century BC. (e) Horseman wearing a hood-like *bashlyk*, short tunic and trousers and armed with a spear in his left hand, who is depicted on a gold disc from the Oxus Treasure (cat no 36), 5th century BC (all the above drawings after Zeimal' Ye V *Amudar'inskii klad*. Leningrad, 1979). (f) Four-horse chariot, not for battle use, with a driver and passenger; a gold model from the Oxus Treasure, 5th century BC (drawing after Curtis J, 1989, ill on front cover). (g) Fragmentary depiction of a rider (Massagetic or Daha), he and his horse both fully armoured, on a terracotta flask piece discovered at Khumbuz-tepe in Southern Khorezmia; 4th - early 3rd century BC (after Mambetullaev M in *Sovetskaya Arkheologiya* 1977, no 3, Fig 1 opp. p.128).

Figure 5: (a) Gold sheath cover for a short sword-*acinaces*, decorated with embossed scenes of a royal lion hunt in the Assyrian style, from the Oxus Treasure; Median or Early Achaemenid work, 6th century BC (drawing after Curtis J, 1989, ill 60). (b) Ivory *acinaces*-sheath from the Oxus Temple at Takht-i Sangin, 5th century BC (drawing after Litvinskiy B A, Pichikiyan I R, 1981, pl I). (c, d) Ivory hilt covers of swords-*acinacae*, provided with roundish slots in order to be fastened to the sword-tangs; from Takht-i Sangin, 5th-4th century BC (drawings after Zeimal' Ye V and others, 1985, cat nos 184 and 190).

Figure 6: (a) Bronze cauldron-shaped helmet of the so-called "Kuban" type, found in 1953 at Samarkand; 6th-5th century BC; note that its lower edge is provided with holes, three on each side and two on the rear, which must have been destined to attaching an aventail of scale armour (drawing after Kuz'mina E E in *Sovetskaya Arkheologiya* 1958, Fig. 1 at p.121). (b-e) Pick-like battle-axes with straight spikes of iron (*chekans*), discovered in Saca graves of the Eastern Pamirs; 5th-3rd century BC (after Litvinskii BA *Drevnie kochevniki "Kryshi mira"*. Moskva, 1972, pl 43,3,4,7,8). (f, g) Eastern Iranians, armed with daggers and "Scythian"-type bows, depicted on an impression of an Achaemenid seal-cylinder of chalcedony from the Oxus Treasure (cat no 114); late 5th-4th century BC (drawing after Dalton O M, 1905). (h) Schematic reconstruction of the "Scythian" bow, shown in unstrung, strung and drawn positions (after Brown F E, 1937, Fig 3a). (i, j) Scythian archers as represented in Greek art (after Chernenko Ye V, 1981, figs 77 and 93).

Figure 7: (a) Alexander the Great depicted as wearing a lion-scalp helmet - the well-known attribute of the mighty hero Heracles' image - on a fragment of a miniature Greek *machaera*-sheath of ivory, found at the Oxus Temple of Takht-i Sangin, 3rd century BC. It seems doubtless that even if such a helmet were in existence, it would be used solely as a parade headgear, but never as a real head-protector for combat. (b) Painted alabaster head of a personage dressed in a *bashlyk*-type cap from Takht-i Sangin, 4th century BC; he seems identical with Vakhsuvar, a Bactrian governor who ruled just before the Seleucid conquest (see Fig 7f). (Drawings after Litvinskiy BA, Pichikiyan I R, 1981, pls VIII and IV respectively). (c) Coin portrait of Sophytes, the ruler of a region in the Oxus valley, late 4th century BC (drawing after Gardner P, 1886, pl I,3). His helmet belongs to the Hellenistic "Attic" type, those with forehead peaks (see Waurick G, 1988, pp.169-173). (d) Graeco-Bactrian king Euthydemus I (about 230-200 BC), wearing a broad-brimmed casque of the "topi" type; a marble bust which is thought to have come from Magnesia on the Meander (in Asia Minor), Euthydemus' native city (drawing after Delbrück R *Antike Porträts*. Bonn; Oxford; Rome, 1912, pl 29). (e) Coin portrait of the Graeco-Bactrian sovereign Antimachus I Theos (about 185-170 BC) shown in a *kausia* - the typical Macedonian beret-like headgear (drawing after Bopearachchi O, 1991, pl 10, ser 1/7), which usually consisted of a leather facing and felt lining; it could be used as both a helmet and an everyday hat (see Saatsoglou-Paliadeli C in *Journal of Hellenic Studies* CXIII, 1993, pp.122-142). (f,g) depictions on a coin of Vakhshuvar who may have been a pre-Seleucid ruler in Bactria; compare his obverse portrait (f) with Fig 7b (drawings after Gardner P in the *Numismatic Chronicle* 1879, pl 1,2).

Figure 8: (a) Iron *sarissa*-head, (b) iron butt-spike of a *sarissa*, both found within the ancient cemetery at Vergina (Greek Macedonia) and dated to Hellenistic times (after Andronicos M in *Bulletin de Correspondance Hellenique* XCIV/1, 1970, fig 9a,c). (c) Greek sword-hilt of ivory shaped into the griffin's head, from Takht-i Sangin, late 4th - 3rd centuries BC (see pictures of similar hilts on Figs 23s, t and

24e, f). (d) Fragmentary Greek sword-hilt of ivory with the image of Heracles, of the same date and location (drawings after Zeimal' Ye V and others, 1985, cat nos 185 and 187). (e-l) Drawings of weaponry belonging to the Dioscuri depicted on coins of the Graeco-Bactrian king Eucratides the Great (about 170-145 BC), which are kept in the American Numismatic Society (in New York) and have been observed by the present author in 1993: (e-g) helmets; (h-j) heads of *sarissae*; (k, l) butt-spikes of *sarissae* (on the coin type with the Dioscuri see Fig 19b). (m) Decorative garniture of an oval shield, discovered at the Arsenal of Ai Khanum, about 150 BC. This garniture, keeping some traces of a human figure probably standing in full face, has survived only as a painted plaster pellicle. It had originally been laid on the shield cover made of leather or wood, but by now lost (after Bernard P and others, 1980, pl XXIII).

Figure 9: Types of weaponry heads from the Arsenal of Ai Khanum, about 150 BC (after Bernard P and others, 1980, pls. XXI and XXII) - (a) iron socketed arrow or javelin head with a rhombic section point; (b-g) iron tanged arrowheads: (b,c) bilobate, (d, f) trilobate, (e) three-sided and (g) four-sided; (h-l) bronze trilobate arrowheads with sockets of two kinds: (h, i) projecting and (j, l) concealed.

Figure 10: Iron weapons discovered at the "Temple with indented niches" of Ai Khanum, 3rd to mid-2nd century BC (after Francfort H-P, 1984, pl 24) - (a, b) fragments of two one-edged blades from swords; (c) lance- or spearhead with a socket and round section point; (d-f) spear- or javelin-heads with sockets and square section points; (g, h) bilobate socketed lance-heads; (i, j) trilobate and tanged arrowheads; (k, m) bilobate and tanged arrowheads; (l) tanged arrow- or javelin-head with a round section point.

Figure 11: (a-l) Weapons found at the Administrative Quarter and the Propylée Area of Ai Khanum, 3rd to mid-2nd century

BC (after Bernard P and others, 1973, Fig 41) - (a) bronze bilobate arrowhead with a projecting socket; (b) bronze trilobate arrowhead with a projecting socket; (c-e) bronze trilobate arrowheads with concealed sockets; (f) iron tanged arrowhead with an oval section point; (g) iron trilobate and tanged arrowhead; (h) bone bilobate and tanged arrowhead; (i) flat point from a flinty arrowhead; (j-l) iron spear- or javelinheads with sockets and four-sided section points. (m-cc) Armament items from the Palace Treasure-House of Ai Khanum, constructed about 150 BC (after Rapin C, 1992, pl 65) - (m-p) iron plates from horse-armour (?); (q,v) iron trilobate arrowheads, their tangs being broken; (r) bronze bilobate and tanged arrowheads; (s) bone bilobate and tanged arrowhead; (t) iron flat point of an arrow; (u) iron socketed trident; (w, x) iron arrowheads with tangs and square section points; (y) iron three-sided arrowhead with a broken tang; (z, aa) iron socketed javelinheads with four-sided section points; (bb) iron socketed arrowhead with a rhombic section point; (cc) iron tanged arrow- or javelinhead with a square section point.

Figure 12: (a-l) Ivory details of scabbards of Greek swords found at the Oxus Temple of Takht-i Sangin, 3rd-2nd century BC (drawings after Pichkyan I R in *Problemy antichnoi kul'tury*, ed by G A Koshelenko. Moskva, 1986, Figs 3-5) - (a-d) scabbard-tops thought to have belonged to the *machaerae*, single-edged and slightly curved slashing weapons; (e-h) scabbard tops of the *xiphoi*, short and straight thrusting swords; (i-l) scabbard-chapes. (m, o) Ivory scabbard-tops of *machaerae* excavated at the "Temple of the Dioscuri" in Dil'berjin, 2nd century BC (drawings after Kruglikova I T, 1986, Fig 24,4,5). (n) Ivory scabbard-top of a *machaera* from the "Temple with indented niches" of Ai Khanum, 3rd to mid-2nd century BC (after Francfort H-P, 1984, pl 10, no 23). (p) Iron double-edged sword, found in pieces, but restored, at the Khalchayan palace building; its total length is 54cm, its blade being 48cm long; the broadest width of the blade is 3.5 cm (after Pugachenkova G A, *Khalchayan*. Tashkent, 1966, pp 53, 56, fig 30). Note how similar this sword is to the typical Greek hoplite *xiphos*. Since the Khalchayan palace was built within the Yuh-chih period this suggests that the sword was either an old trophy or was made in imitation of an older type and utilised by the Yüeh-chih as an infantry weapon.

Figure 13: (a) Bronze fragment of a cuirass from the citadel of Kampyr-tepe, about mid-2nd century BC (after Nikonorov V P, Savchuk S A, 1992, Fig 1). (b-e) Armour set of iron for the *cataphractarius*, from the Arsenal of Ai Khanum, about 150 BC (drawings after Bernard P and others, 1980, pls XXXVII and XXXVIII) - (b) horse piece of defence thought to have been either a plastron (Bernard P in *Comptes rendus des séances de l'Académie des inscriptions et belles lettres* 1980, p.455) or the flank-guard covering also a horseman's leg, called by Xenophon *parameridia* (Grenet F in Bernard P and others, 1980, p.61; see about this element of armour in Chapter 2 in connection with considering the cavalryman on Fig. 4g); (c) trooper's corselet portion composed of scales, each measuring 5.3 x 4.5 cm; (d) left leg-guard consisting of annular straps joined so that the lower one slightly overlaps the upper; in other words, here we deal with the actual hooped tube-like protector used for both the legs and arms, the earliest Central Asian representations of which are shown on Fig 4c,g; in this case the device is additionally provided with such important protective elements for the rider as a semi-cylindrical plate covering the thigh (right) and a curved piece topping the foot (left); (e) pair of shoulder-pieces, found positioned one on the other, each of them being composed of three parts: a completion of lanceolate scales protecting the shoulder-blade, four rectangular lamellae covering transversally the shoulder top and an oblong plate provided with a buckle permitting the attachment to the corselet.

Figure 14: (a, b) Types of stone balls and bullets discovered at the Citadel of Ai Khanum, about 150 BC (drawings after Leriche P, 1986, photos 27 and 28). (c) Iron elephant-goad (*ank*) from the "Temple with indented niches" of Ai Khanum, 3rd to mid-2nd century BC (after Francfort H-P, 1984, pl 25, no 6). (d,e) Iron elephant-goads found at Taxila, respectively one from the Bhir Mound, 3rd-2nd century BC, and the other from Sirkap, 1st century BC to 1st century AD (drawings after Marshall J, 1951, pl 170, nos 101 and 102).

Figure 15: Bactrian horse-furniture from Ai Khanum, 3rd to 2nd century BC - (a, b) Iron snaffle-bits of two sections jointed in middle, with rings intended for the attachment of the reins and cheek-bars or mouthguards to prevent the rein from slipping into the horse's mouth. (c,d) Two types of mouthguards, respectively a "propeller-shaped one and one with the inferior extremity curved under the horse's lower jaw. (e-i) discs-*phalerae* to ornament the trappings, those (e, g, i) being of bronze and (f, h) of iron. After: (a) - Bernard P and others, 1973, Fig 43; (b-i) Guillaume O in *L'archéologie de la Bactriane ancienne*. Paris, 1985, Figs 7-9, 11-15.

Figure 16: (a,b) Graeco-Bactrian war-elephants depicted on silver *phalerae* dating from about 200 BC, now in the Hermitage, Sankt-Petersburg (drawings after Trever K V, 1940, pls 1 and 2); see in detail our Pl 2. (c) Coin portrait of the Graeco-Bactrian king Demetrius I (about 22-190 BC), a pioneer of conquering North-Western India; his elephant-scalp headgear may have commemorated this event (drawing after Bopearachchi O, 1991, pl 4, ser 1/3). (d) Bronze figurine of a rider wearing an elephant-scalp headpiece, now in the Metropolitan Museum, New York; found in Egypt, it may represent either Demetrius I of Bactria or one of the local monarchs from the Ptolemaic dynasty (drawing after Sekunda N, 1994, Fig 50). True, there is an opinion that the elephant-scalp on Demetrius' portrayals had no connection with his Indian conquests, but was rather a symbol of power extended far eastwards, to India, in imitation of the same headdress of Alexander the Great known on early Ptolemaic and Seleucid coins (see Tarn W W, 1985, p.131).

Figure 17: Four views of a helmeted head of painted clay, discovered in 1984 among other sculptural fragments which were buried in the Square Hall Building of the famous Parthian fortress of Old Nisa, situated near Ashgabad in Southern Turkmenistan (drawings after Pilipko V N in *Vestnik Drevnei Istorii* 1989, no 3, Figs 2-8). It is not yet evident, who could be depicted here, but in any case he is not anyone from the midst of the Parthian Arsacids. It seems more probable that this personage is a Seleucid king or governor However that might be, worthy of notice is the helmet depicted, belonging to the "Attic"-type with forehead peaks, which were used in Early Hellenistic Bactria as well (see Fig 7c). Note that the cheek-pieces of the helmet are decorated with the so-called "bundle of lightning" design widely spread in the Hellenistic world.

Figure 18: (a) Coin of the Indo-Greek ruler Agathocles (about 190-180 BC), representing Zeus armed with a lightning bolt and shield shaped into a human guise. (b) Coin of the Graeco-Bactrian king Demetrius II (175-170), with the representation of Athena equipped with a brimmed casque going back to the "Boeotian" helmets (see on them Waurick G, 1988, pp.159-163), a spear and round convex shield. (c) Coin of the Indo-Greek sovereign Apollodotus I (about 180-160 BC), showing Athena Nikephora with a crested and peaked helmet as well as a round shield. (d) Another coin of Apollodotus I, with Apollo holding a "segment"-type bow and arrow (drawings after Bopearachchi O, 1991, respectively pls 8, ser 14/F; 14, ser 1/2; 11, ser 1/A; 14 ser 6/99).

Figure 19: (a-c) Pictures on coins of Eucratides I the Great (about 170-145 BC), showing this Graeco-Bactrian king himself in a late form of the "Boeotian"-type helmet with a crest-plume (a, c), as well as the charging Heavenly twins Dioscuri who wear "Pilos"-type helmets (see on them Waurick G, 1988, pp.151-158) and carry very long lances-*sarissae* in one hand (see a reconstruction on Pl 3B). (d) Coin of the Indo-Greek ruler Antimachus II Nicephorus (about 160-155 BC), representing him as a cavalryman (see in detail Pl 3D). (e) Coin of the Graeco-Bactrian sovereign Eucratides II (about 145-140 BC), with the image of Apollo holding a "segment" bow and arrow (drawings after Bopearachchi O, 1991, respectively pls 16, ser 4/25; 19, ser 8/56; 15, ser 1/11; 22, ser 1/5). (f,g) Depictions on a coin of a Graeco-Bactrian king Plato (about 145 - 140); he is shown himself on the obverse wearing a Graeco-Bactrian version of the "Boeotian" helmet similar to that of Eucratides the Great; on the reverse is pictured Helios, the god of the Sun, in the radiant nimbus, riding a four-horse chariot (quadrigae) with patterned box-like body (drawings after Bopearaschchi O, 1991, pl 24, ser 3/B).

Figure 20: (a-d) Representations on coins of the great Indo-Greek king Menander I the Saviour (about 155-130 BC), where he is wearing a helmet which seems to go back to the "Boeotian" type, but with some slight changes, namely its rear part is lower and topping either is covered by scales or imitates curly hair (a, c); his corselet is made of scales (a, d), the offensive arm is a javelin (d). Athena Alkidemos on his coins (b) has a "Boeotian" helmet too, as well as a scaled chest-piece and round convex shield armoured by scales. (e) Coin of the Indo-Greek ruler Lysias (about 120-110 BC) in a helmet like that of Menander. Drawings after: (a, b) - Gardner P, 1886, pl XI,8; (c-e) - Bopearachchi O, 1991, pls 29, ser 16/103; 26, ser 6/12; 38, ser 2/3)

Figure 21: Pictures on coins of "middle" Indo-Greek sovereigns - (a) Antialcidas (about 115-95 BC); (b, c) Philoxenus (about 100-95 BC); (d, e) Amyntas (about 95-90 BC). They all wear local interpretations of "Boeotian" helmets of ; in two cases (b, e) scaled corselets are visible, in one (d) - perhaps a cuirass (drawings after Bopearachchi O, 1991, pls 39, ser 3/2; 43, ser 1/1; 44, ser 10/D; 46, ser 1/B; 47, ser 10/G).

Figure 22: Depictions on coins of later Indo-Greek rulers - (a) Portrait of Archebius (about 90-80 BC) dressed in a local "Boeotian"-type helmet and scaled corselet; the clear line of his cheek creates a false illusion of the presence of a cheek-piece, though such a device which was not a distinctive feature of the "Boeotian" headpieces. (b) Hermaeus (about 90-70 BC) pictured as a rider wearing a "Boeotian" helmet too and armed with a spear attached behind his back and a bow in a quiver or open bowcase-*gorytus*. (c, d) Apollo armed with bows of two types, the first with a "broken" line of the stave (that is either "segment-shaped" or "doubly convex", according to the typology of G Rausing, 1967, p.20 and Fig 5) and the other, probably long and double-arched, with long and straight ears, on pieces of Apollodotus II (about 80-65 BC). (e) Hippostratus (about 65-55 BC) as a mounted warrior outfitted with a "Boeotian"-style helmet, cuirass (?) and thigh-protector in the shape of an armoured skirt. Drawings after: (a-c, e) Bopearachchi O, 1991, pls 50, ser 1/1; 52, ser 1/1; 63, ser 16/37; 65, ser 5/6; (d) Gardner P, 1886, pl X,6.

Figure 23: (a-p) Drawings of weapons represented on the Graeco-Bactrian and Indo-Greek coins (after Srivastava A K *Catalogue of Indo-Greek Coins in the State Museum, Lucknow. Lucknow*, 1969, Figs 13-28) - (a, b) bows, respectively of the "segment" and "Scythian" types; (c, d) arrows; (e) open *gorytus* with a bow inside; (f-j) shields: note those (f, g) provided with round bosses and (i, j) decorated with human guises, the latter having such as the boss; (k-p) examples of tridents, lances, javelins and spears. (q-oo) Drawings of arms and armour depicted on the celebrated ivory drinking horns (Greek *rhyta*), dating from 2nd century BC, recovered at the Treasure-House of Old Nisa (after Masson M Ye, Bugachenkova G A *Parfyanskie ritony Nisy*. Ashkhabad, 1959, Figs 17b, 27-29, 31, 35) - (q) armed personage from the *rhyton* no 30, who wears a brimmed and spiked helmet of the late "Boeotian" style, plain cuirass, skirt-shaped thigh-protector armoured by two rows of oblong plates, boots and holds a spear and sheathed sword-*machaera* suspended by means of the shoulder-strap; (r) spear; (s-y) Greek swords of the *machaera* (chiefly) and *kopis* (v) types, two of them (s, t) having the griffin-shaped hilts like that from Takht-i Sangin (Fig 8c; see also 24e, f); (z-bb) bows of the "Scythian" type; (cc) "Scythian" bow placed in an open *gorytus*; (dd-gg) pole-axes; (hh-oo) helmets which, except for a plumed casque (hh) and an unusual headpiece shaped into a gable roof (jj), seem to go back to the "Boeotian" type, but with variously formed tops. It should be noted that the Nisean *rhyta* are sometimes postulated as Parthian by their origin, but proceeding, in fact, only from the place of their finding. However, it seems much more probable that they belonged to Graeco-Bactrian works of art, as some outstanding researchers of Hellenistic and Iranian art have supposed on the grounds of the fact that the decorations of these vessels are basically Greek, but not Oriental (see Ghirshman R, 1962, p.30; Barnett R D in *Iranica Antiqua* VIII, 1968, p.49; Bernard P in *Journal des Savants* 1985, pp.89-91). These splendid ivories could have been brought to Old Nisa's Treasure-House as spoils after the successful war of the Parthian monarch Mithridates I against his Graeco-Bactrian colleague Eucratides I, which took place about 150 BC. And so one may consider the weaponry pictured on the Nisean *rhyta* as reflecting not Parthian, but Graeco-Bactrian warfare.

Figure 24: (a) Terracotta plaque from the citadel of Kampyr-tepe, found in a context dating to the first half of 2nd century BC, which depicts a well-armed warrior standing under an arch (after Nikonorov V P, Savchuk S A, 1992, p.50, Fig 2); see Pl 3A as his reconstruction. G A Pugachenkova (in *Obshchestvennye nauki v Uzbekistane* 1989, no 4, pp.55-57) has expressed an opinion that this is the image of a Roman solider on the plaque belonging to the first half of 2nd century AD (?). Her conclusion cannot be accepted, above all because of the above archaeological context of this find. On the other hand, the warrior's outfit assemblage - a spiked helmet, plain cuirass, typical Greek thigh-defence called *pteryges* which consists of narrow strips made up in two rows (the upper one being much shorter than the lower), large oval shield going back to the *thyreos* type, and finally distinctive Greek straight sword-*xiphos* with a short blade of the stretched rhombic form - appears to be of Hellenistic rather than of Roman inspiration. (b) Terracotta figurine of 2nd century BC from Begram, representing an Indo-Greek soldier with a typical large oval *thyreos* (after Ghirshman R. *Begram*. Le Caire, 1946, pl XXVIII, no 539). Such shields consisted usually of a framework made of wooden planks, long vertical and short horizontal, covered by leather and provided with a longitudinal metal spindle-shaped boss for rigidity of the whole construction; this boss is well visible on the Begram terracotta, whereas on the piece from Kampyr-tepe (a) it is replaced by a massive metal lizard-like emblem carrying the same function. The shields-*thyreoi*, thought to have been invented in Central Italy during the Early Iron Age and then adopted by the Trans-Alpine Celts (see Stary P F in *Proceedings of the Prehistoric Society* 45, 1979, p.200), were brought to the Near East by the Celts-Galatians intruding into Asia Minor in 3rd century BC, as a number of relevant pictorial evidences from there demonstrate (see Sekunda N, 1994, Figs 21, 23, 24, 35, 46, 47, 54). Not later than within 2nd century BC these shields reached the Middle East as well. (c-e) Pieces of art of probable Graeco-Bactrian origin, dating from 2nd century BC, which have been found in much later Yüeh-chih rich graves of the Tillya-tepe necropolis (drawings after Sarianidi V I *Bactrian Gold from the Excavations of the Tillya-tepe Necropolis in Northern Afghanistan*. Leningrad, 1985, ills 69, 73, 81-84) - (c) cameo from Grave no 4, with the portrait of a Graeco-Bactrian king in a helmet of the "Boeotian" type (compare Fig 19a, c); (d) pendant from Grave no 3, with the picture of Athena wearing a "Boeotian"-style headpiece and carrying a spear and round shield with a pyramid-shaped boss crowned by a small ball; (e, f) warriors represented on gold clasps from Grave no 3 (see Pl 3C as their summarised reconstruction); it should be additionally noted here that firstly, their helmets provided with cheek-pieces go back rather to the "Attic" peaked headpieces than to the "Boeotian"; secondly, their thigh-protector is an armoured skirt like that on Fig 23q; thirdly, they wear light trousers tied up with narrow clasped straps under the knees.

Figure 25: (a) Iron shield-boss from the citadel of Kampyr-tepe, discovered in a context dating from 2nd century BC, but before the Yüeh-chih invasion. (b) Iron axe from the same place, 2nd to 1st century BC (drawings received by courtesy of S A Savchuk) (c) Silver, partially gilt, parade battle-axe with a curved blade (*klevets*) from the Treasure-House of Old Nisa, late 2nd to early 1st century BC (drawing after a photograph kindly granted by A B Nikitin). Although found in Parthia, this weapon seems to be of Central Asian steppe origin. The fact is that such battle-axes, primarily destined to pierce armour, are depicted as symbols of power (like the luxuriously ornamented one shown) on coins of the Indo-Saca and Early Kushan rulers (Figs 26b and 37d). The Nisean exemplar may have been captured by the Parthians during the struggle which was conducted by the Arsacid king Mithridates II (123-88 BC) in the east of his empire against the Saca and Tocharian hordes moving westwards after the fall of Greek Bactria. (d) Draft of Tomb 1, constructed of mud bricks in the Fortification area of Ai Khanum by later occupants (the Yüeh-chih?), 1st century BC (e, f) Iron arms belonging to the dead person of Tomb 1, respectively a knife and dagger, the latter having been found in a wooden sheath, from which three pearls, one of agate two of white stone, have also survived (after Leriche P, 1986, p.110, Figs 52 and 54).

Figure 26: (a, b) Coins of the Indo-Saca king Spalirises (first quarter of 1st century BC) showing him as both the fully armoured *cataphractarius* and dismounted, with a *klevets* (see Fig 25c) and "Scythian"-style bow. (c, d) Coins of one of Spalirises' successors, Azes I (around mid-1st century BC) depicting him as a *cataphractarius* as well. Drawings after: (a) - Bivar A D H, 1972, Fig 1a; (b-d) - Gardner P, 1886, respectively pls XXII,2, XVII,8, XVII,4

Figure 27: Yüeh-chih mounted archers in hunting episodes engraved on ivory casket panels from the Oxus Temple of Takht-i Sangin, 1st century BC - early 1st century AD (after Litvinskiy B A, Pichikiyan I R, 1981, pl. VII, as well as the same authors in *Pamyatniki Kul'tury. Novye otkrytiya. Yezhegodnik 1983*. Leningrad, 1985, fig at p. 515); see Pl 4A reconstructing the horseman (a). Attracting our attention are their bows provided with very long ears. At present, they may be the earliest representations of bows belonging to a type which is only conditionally called "Sasanian" (see Fig 44 m-o) owing to a number of Sasanian-style silver vessels bearing depictions of such long-eared shooting weapons. One can see that our riders carry the bows of two stave configurations - with a clear two-arched outline (b) and without it (a, c); note also that in the latter case the bows are obviously asymmetrical, with the upper arms longer than the lower ones - to facilitate more accurate shooting.

Figure 28: (a) Schematic engraving on a bone from Kala-i Mir (in the Lower Kafirnigan valley, also named Kobadian, within Southern Tajikistan), representing a warrior dressed in what may be interpreted as a laminar casque and long armoured coat made rather of quilted leather than of metal scales; late 2nd - 1st century BC (after Staviskii B Ya *Kushanskaya Baktriya*. Moskva, 1977, fig 38). (b) Engraving on a bone plate, found at the Kuyumazar cemetery (in the Bukhara oasis of Sogdia), with the picture of a nomadic newcomer wearing a quilted body-armour too; 2nd to 1st century BC (after Stawiski B *Kunst der Kuschan (Littelasien)*. Leipzig, 1971, fig at p. 70). See a corselet of the same style on a later relief from Gandhara (Fig 42f). (c-e) Clay fragmentary sculpture from the palace building at Khalchayan, early 1st century AD - (c) male personage with a corselet (see Fig 30g); (d) warrior's head in a tight-fitting helmet with a forehead peek (see Fig 30a, and Pl 4C for its detailed description); (e) female personage (Athena?) wearing a casque with a brim broken off (drawings after: (c,e) Bugachenkova G A, 1971, Ills 61, 88; (d) the same author, 1979, ill 119).

Figure 29: (a-d) Fragments of sculptural representations of horses and light archers from the Khalchayan palace. (e-g) Reconstructions of horse-furniture parts depicted at Khalchayan (after Bugachenkova G A, 1971, figs at pp. 68-71). (h) Fragment from the same place, showing a unique saddle of a rigid framework, provided with both the front and rear arches (after Pugachenkova G A. *Khalchayan*. Tashkent, 1966, fig 95). See Fig 31a and Pl 4B.

Figure 30: Sculptural fragments from Khalchayan, depicting armour for both a *cataphractarius* and his horse - (a) helmet; (b, g) corselets; (c) horse protective mask; (d) horse neck-defence; (e, f) rider's leg- and arm-guards respectively. See in detail our reconstruction on Pl 4C and compare it with Fig 31a, b. Drawings after: (a, c-e) -

Pugachenkova G A in *Vestnik Drevnei Istorii* 1966, no. 2, figs 11 and 12; (b, f, g) - the same author, 1971, respectively figs at pp. 66, 60 and ill 62.

Figure 31: Reconstructions of the sculptural compositions and their personages, ornamenting the Khalchayan palace, as proposed by G A Pugachenkova (1971, respectively figs at pp 71, 72, 51 and 61).

Figure 32: High rank Yüeh-chih persons, buried in graves nos 2 and 4 of the Tillya-tepe necropolis and their equipment; first half of 1st century AD - (a) Dagger, with overall length 37.5 cm, from grave No. 5. It has an iron double-edged blade, lozenge-shaped in its cross-section, and is richly decorated, with both cross-guard and pommel hilt; the latter is faced by a gold plating and encrusted with turquoise beads. The dagger was found in a wooden, leather-covered sheath, which is also mounted with a gold plating with turquoise insets; relievo ornaments on both the hilt and sheath reproduce one and the same basic motif, namely the mauling of beasts. The sheath is provided with four rounded projections, of which two lower, both holed (unlike the upper without any holes), are intended for its attachment to the thigh. (b) Sheath from the same burial, being a gold-mounted bronze plate with two rounded projections at its bottom; its gold facing, encrusted by turquoise insets, is embellished with longitudinal swastika ornaments along the edges and with the relievo depiction of two fantastic creatures mauling each other. This sheath contained three knives with iron blades and ivory hilts, the main of which - single-edged, with overall length 23 cm - was inserted into the central, convex, portion of the obverse (its hilt is visible), whereas another two, smaller ones could be located in a leather etwee on the back of the sheath. (c-e) Gold, ornamented in the animal style, plaques thought to have belonged to the horse-trappings, from the same burial. (f,g) Drafts of Graves Nos 4 and 2 respectively

(after Sarianidi V I. *Khram i nekropol' Tillyatepe*. Moskva, 1989, respectively figs 33,1,2, 34,1, 35,1-3, 30,2, 16,1). (h,i) Persons from Graves Nos 4 and 2, reconstructed and drawn by S A Yatsenko. The former is a prince wearing a parade headgear decorated on the top with gold sculptures of a tree and mountain ram, as well as typical Yüeh-chih/Kushan garb consisting of a belted caftan, wrapped over to the left, and wide trousers-*sharovary* (see Fig 36b, d and Pl 5B). Buried probably in the winter time, he had mittens as well. All the articles of his garb were richly decorated with a great number of small gold plaques. The dead man was outfitted with the above bladed weapons (a,b), which were attached to the thighs by means of narrow straps both passing through the lower projections of the sheaths and being fastened to the top of their back. It is also reported that a long sword was uncovered with him, but it is still unpublished. The latter person (i) is a princess also dressed in very embellished garments. She is shown here holding a pick-like axe, with an iron blade, which was detected in a wicker basket situated near her feet.

Figure 33: Iron weapons (a-p) and metal belt-buckles (q-u) from graves of the Tulkhar cemetery in the Bishkent valley; last third of 2nd century BC to early 1st century AD (after Mandel'shtam A M. *Kochevniki na puti v Indiyu*. Moskva and Leningrad, 1966, pp 102-114, pls XXXIX-XLIV) - (a, b) Long, double-edged swords with metal straight cross-guards; judging by some organic remains revealed on their blades and hilt-tangs, they were inserted into wooden scabbards, which had originally been stained in bright red colour and painted with black ornamentation, and their hilt-covers, being also of wood, were attached to the tangs by iron rivets; the hilt of the exemplar (b) seems to have been crowned by a small ball-shaped pommel of wood, whereas nearby the end of the blade of the other (a) some traces of a copper or bronze scabbard-chape have been brought to light. (c-i) Double-edged daggers, provided with both metal straight cross-guards, one (i) having it destroyed, and metal pommels of various configurations, namely those shaped into a "sickle" (c), "heart" (d-g: see also Fig 25f), "volute" (h) and "bar" (i); as a rule, on their blades some vestiges of wooden sheaths have been revealed, which were adorned like those of the above swords. Tanged arrowheads: (j-m) trilobate and (n-p) three-edged. Buckles: (q) figured, of brass; (r, s) ring-shaped, of iron; (t, u) plate-type, of iron.

Figure 34: (a-i) Types of iron tanged arrowheads found at Dil'berjin, 1st century BC - 1st century AD (after Kruglikova I T, 1986, fig 35b) - (a, c) three-sided, (b, g-i) trilobate, (d, f) bilobate, (e) bullet-shaped. (j-m) Iron bladed weapons from graves of the Babashov cemetery (in North-Western Bactria); 1st-2nd century AD (after Mandel'shtam A M. *Pamyatniki kochevnikov kushanskogo vremeni v Severnoi Baktrii*. Leningrad, 1975, p 114, pl XXX) - (j) Two-edged dagger with both metal cross-guard and metal, but destroyed, pommel; (k, l) two-edged daggers without metal cross-guards and pommels. All these daggers were carried in wooden sheaths, from which some remain, stained in red colour and painted with black ornaments, have survived. (m) Long, double-edged sword lacking both metal cross-guard and pommel; it was purposely bent before placement into the grave, in accordance with some funeral rite. The cross-guards and pommels of those (k-m) were certainly made of wood hence have not survived. It should be noted that the Central Asian swords and daggers lacking metal cross-guards and pommels are usually thought to be later than those provided with them, and they have to be dated to the time after the commencement of the Christian Era. (n-s) Armament items from a catacomb grave of Barrow no 2 of the Orlat cemetery in the region of Samarkand (in Sogdia); 1st to 3rd century AD - (n) iron two-edged dagger (or short sword) provided with disc-pommel of marmoreal stone (o)

and cross-guard of jade (p); (q) scabbard-slide of jade; (r, s) handle- and (t, u) end-covers of bone for a bow (after Pugachenkova G A. *Drevnosti Miankalya*. Tashkent, 1989, fig 56).

Figure 35: (a-o) Armour and horse-harness from the site of Sirkap at Taxila, 1st century AD (after Marshall J, 1951, pls 165, nos. 93, 94, 96-98, 100a,b; 170, nos 90-92, 99; 200, nos 115-117) - (a, b) Two groups of arm-guards of iron, intended for a *cataphractarius*; they are described by the excavator (p 550) only as composed of "twenty-four and eighteen pieces respectively, of varying sizes and shapes", however, their construction, even for lack of more detailed description, seems to have borne resemblance to that of the hooped tube-like arm- and leg-protectors well known thanks to both the actual (Fig 13d) and illustrative (Figs 4c,g, 26a,c,d, 28c, 30f,g, 38c, 39c,d, 40, 45a) sources. (c) Iron helmet with a cheek-piece on its one surviving side, which is most likely attached by a pivot permitting it to be raised or lowered; the helmet, measuring 23.75 cm length, 17.5cm width and 15 cm height, had first been forged from one metal piece shaped into an oval bowl and then was reinforced by means of horizontal bands hammered onto it; its summit was provided with a boss for the attachment of a crest, plume or spike. (d, e) Iron discs, 4.7 cm and 7.1 cm in diameter respectively, fitted with staples at their backs as the attachment means, which both, though believed by J Marshall (p 550) to have been shield-bosses (*umbones*), seem to have served rather as *phalerae* of the horse-trappings. (f) Iron plate, measuring about 25 x 21.25 x 2 cm, from an armour set of eighteen big plates, curved to fit the body and varying sizes and patterns; proceeding from their dimensions and heavy weight, this set must have belonged to an armoured trapper of a horse or even of an elephant (see Fig 42a). (g-i) Iron snaffle-bits, jointed in middle. (j-l) Iron cheek-bars (mouthguards), each being provided with two staples for fastening, of two configurations: straight (j, k) and S-shaped (l). (m-o) Cheek-bars of horn (m) and bone (n, o), each fitted with two holes to fix an iron staple holding the ringed bit (see Marshall J, 1951, pl 205b). (p-s) Iron plates and scales that appear to have belonged to a composed-type helmet, found at Shaikhan Dheri, Charsada (Pakistan), in a context dating from the reign of the Kushan king Vasudeva, that is within the first quarter of the 3rd century AD (after Allchin F R in *Journal of the Royal Asiatic Society of Great Britain and Ireland* 1970, pp 113-120, fig 1). (t) Reconstruction of this helmet proposed by M V Gorelik (1982, p 103, pl 11), according to whom, its cupola-shaped body was composed of narrow vertical plates, enveloped from below by a metal band and covered from above by a metal crown-piece; from the rear it was provided with an aventail of metal laminae.

Figure 36: Minor works of art from Kampyr-tepe (a-e) and the Termez Museum (f) - (a) Terracotta statuette depicting a sitting ruler, late 2nd - 1st century BC. (b) Bronze buckle portraying a rider, dressed in a short, long-sleeved caftan and wide trousers, falling together with his horse; late 2nd - 1st century BC. (c) Terracotta figurine, moulded in low relief, of a male, bare-headed personage, standing on a pedestal and encased in a "muscle" cuirass, armoured wide waist-belt and thigh-protector in the shape of an armoured skirt; late 1st - first half of 2nd century AD. (d) Wooden statuette sheathed in a silver facing, representing a bearded man in light garments; first half of 2nd century AD (see Pl 5B reconstructing him). (e) Fragment of a terracotta showing a bearded man in a tall cone-shaped headgear; 1st to 2nd century AD. (f) Terracotta figurine depicting, most likely, the same personage in the same protective equipment as the above terracotta (c), but made in a different mould (see Pl 5C dealing with them). After: (a, c, f) - Nikonorov V P, Savchuk S A, 1992, figs 3-5; drawings (b, d, e) - Pugachenkova G A and others, 1991, cat nos 167, 166, 159.

Figure 37: (a) Depiction on a coin issued by a ruler bearing two names or titles - "Sanab" and "Heraos", who reigned over one of the five Yüeh-chih principalities (Chinese *Hsi-hou* or *yabgu*), namely that called Kuei-shuang (Kushan), around the commencement of the Christian Era; here shown is a rider carrying a long *gorytus*-type device which consists of two sections - a bow-case (rather of soft material like leather) to keep the unstrung bow and quiver to contain the arrows (drawing after Zeimal' Ye V and others, 1985, cat no 102). (b) Silver medallion, now in the Hermitage Museum, with the image of an armed female personage (Kushan goddess Nana?), who has a "Scythian" bow and sword or dagger coming in sight from behind her back; 1st to 3rd century AD (drawing after Trever K V, 1940, pl 12). (c, d) Pictures on the obverse and reverse of a coin minted by an early Kushan ruler of Bactria calling himself "King of Kings, Great Saviour"; about 50 AD (drawings after Gardner P, 1886, pl XXIV,6); here, in consecutive order seen are his bust in a brimmed and plumed helmet of the Graeco-Bactrian/Indo-Greek version of the "Boeotian" headpieces, as well as his equestrian portrait where he is shown wearing a *tiara*-like headgear and scaled corselet (?), and holding a *klevets*. (e) Kushan seal of 2nd century AD from the British Museum, with the representation of a rider, who wears a low cap and holds in the left hand an object that seems to be a pick-like battle axe with a straight spike (*chekan* - see Fig 6b-e); especially deserving attention is the fact that this personage seems to have a hook-like foot support, going down from his saddle - such a device could be a forerunner of the real stirrup invented roughly two centuries later. The above dating of the seal is grounded on the analysis of both its one word inscription and monogram belonging to the ruling years of Kanishka I and Nuvishka (drawing and description after Rosenfield J M, 1967, pl XVI, pp 101-102). (f) Bronze medallion, found at Zar-tepe (near Termez), with the image of the Great Kushan monarch

Huvishka (second half of 2nd century AD), who is shown wearing a cone-shaped helmet, perhaps of the "spangenhelm" construction, and holding a mace in his left hand (after Zavialov V A in *Sovetskaya Arkheologiya* 1979, no 3, pp 150-151, fig 8).

Figure 38: (a, b) Wall-painting fragments, discovered in a prosperous town-dweller's house at Dal'verzin-tepe, depicting a warrior's head in a helmet, and a horse's head in a mask; second half 1st - 2nd century AD (drawings after Pugachenkova G A and others. *Dal'verzintepe - kushanskii gorod na yuge Uzbekistana.* Tashkent, 1978, pl IV). Both the helmet and mask were painted blue, presumably to represent burnished steel. The helmet, which is provided with cheek-pieces and peak, is composed of horizontal bands, which seem to be riveted to a metal framework; below the headpiece can be seen a row of laminae forming probably the armoured collar of a corselet. Very interesting is the protective horse-mask testifying, along with the fragment from Khalchayan (Fig 30c), to the usage of such a rare piece of armour in Bactria in at least the very early 1st millennium AD. (c) Fragmentary small round object of dark-green nephrite (diameter 6 cm, thickness 8-9 cm), which has recently been found (in 1982) by chance on the surface at Old Termez. On its obverse, concave side is engraved an Indian woman playing the lute, whereas on the other, convex, demonstrated here - is a charging mounted lancer (drawing after Pidaev Sh R in *Obshchestvennye nauki v Uzbekistane* 1990, no 9, pp 37-41, fig 2). He wears a cuirass or sleeveless tunic over a corselet, "hooped" arm-guards, cloak and boots; his weapons are a long lance, apparently the two-handed *contus* rather than one-handed *sarissa*, and long sword suspended on the right (its owner therefore has to be left handed to unsheathe it). This piece of art, in the so-called Gandharan-style must have been exported to Bactria from North-Western India some time between the Kushan invasion of India and the fall of the Great Kushan empire, that is from about 50 to about 250 AD. The horseman's depiction may have been reproduced on the reverse side of the disc not in Gandhara, but after it had already arrived in the Bactrian region. (d) Coin representation of the famous Kushan king Kanishka I (first half of 2nd century AD) standing before an altar. He is armed with a spear and sword, while his garments - a banded cap, long caftan, cloak and trousers-*sharovary* - are purely civilian (drawing after Gardner P, 1886, pl 26,15). (e) Portrait statue of Kanishka I from Mathura (India), which seems to date from the early years of his reign (drawing after Rosenfield J M, 1967, fig 2); see Pl 5A as a reconstruction. (f) Unfinished bas-relief from the famous Kushan dynastic sanctuary at Surkh Kotal near Baghlan (in Southern Bactria, 2nd century AD; its personage has a long sword that was undoubtably intended to be represented as suspended by means of a scabbard-slide (after Rosenfield J M, 1967, fig 123). (g) Lower portion of a portrait statue from the same site, depicting a royal person (Kanishka I?) wearing a long top-caftan, ornate under-tunic and *sharovary*; stuck out is a dagger attached to the waist-belt perhaps by means of a disc on its sheath (after Stawiski B, 1979, fig at p 90).

Figure 39: (a, b) Armed deities of the Kushan pantheon, depicted on coins of Muvishka (second half of 2nd century AD); note their "Indo-Greek" variant of the "Boeotian" helmets, with a low rear part (see Figs 20a,c,e, 21a-c, 22a,e), as well as "muscle" cuirasses and round shields with the variously shaped outsides - "knobby"-like (a) and plain (b). (c) Coin portrait of the king Kanishka II (late 2nd century); see Pl 6A reconstructing his outfit. (d) Coin representation of Hormizd, a Sasanian governor (*Kushanshah*) of the former Kushan empire in around mid-4th century, whose equipment is mainly of Kushano-Bactrian inspiration; see Pl 8A (drawings after Göbl R., 1984, pls 18, no 236; 24, no 332; 51, no 634/6; 63, no 707).

Figure 40: Coin depictions of the Kushan king Vasudeva (first quarter of 3rd century AD), encased in full armour. There are four variants, three (a-c) being reconstructed on Pl 6B-D; the fourth, (d), combines a scaled corselet like Variant (b) and armoured skirt like Variant (a). The helmet might be provided with an aventail (rather than with cheek-pieces). However, a shafted weapon of Variant (d) is not the trident, as in the other cases, but it is fitted with a vague head - maybe, something like a halberd (drawings after Göbl R, 1984, respectively pls 32, no 525; 28, no 501; 50, no 633; 30 no 511).

Figure 41: Items of military equipment on Kushan coins (after Göbl R, 1984, pls IV, VI and 90, no 869/4) - (a-o) Headgear and helmets of (a-c) Vima Kadhises (second half of 1st century AD), (d, e) Kanishka I, (g-k) Huvishka, (l, m) Vasudeva, (n, o) Kanishka II, of which: specimens (a, b, d) made of thick soft material (such as leather or felt) could be of fighting use too; (c, e) metal casques; (f-i) decorated metal helmets of semi-spherical form; (j, k, m, o) *tiara*-like, decorated headpieces of metal or thick soft material; (l, n) helmets, perhaps of the "spangenhelm" construction, with cone-shaped bodies covered by ornamented leather or metal scale-armour. (p, q) Swords with hilt-pommels in the form of a bird's head, Huvishka (compare the sword-hilt on Fig 38e). (r, s) Dagger and sword, Vasudeva; note both triangle-shaped blade and "bar-like" pommel of the former, as well as both round pommel and scabbard-chape of the latter. (t) Sword, similar to (s), Varahran *Kushanshah* (late 3rd - early 4th century). (u, v) Spears with triangle-and leaf-shaped heads, Huvishka). (w-z) Tridents, Vasudeva. (aa) Standard with bird-shaped top, Huvishka. (bb, cc) Standards with wheel- and triple-globe-shaped tops, Vasudeva. (dd, ee) Clubs, Vima Kadphises. (ff, gg) Maces, Huvishka. (hh) King Huvishka riding an elephant with a goad (*ank*). (ii) Elephant-goad held by bust of Huvishka (see also goads in Fig 14c-e).

Figure 42: Depictions in sculpture of the Gandharan school, which flourished in the North-Western Indian region under the Great Kushan kings (late 1st to mid-3rd century AD), dealing with the local actualities of warfare within that epoch - (a-c) Fragments of reliefs of green schist, found at the site of Butkara I (in the Swat valley, Pakistan) (drawings after Faccenna D and others. *Sculptures from the Sacred Area of Butkara I (Swat, W Pakistan).* Pt 3 Roma, 1964, pls CDLXX and CDLXXIII) - (a) War-elephant, covered by a protective trapper composed of big rectangular plates (compare Fig 35f) and carrying on the back a tower, both crenelated and loop-holed, with not less than two warriors inside, and on the neck a mahout as well; take notice of the personage (b) as one of rare representations of armoured cavalrymen in the art of the Kushan period. (d) Fragmentary stucco figure from Hadda (Southern Afghanistan), wearing a cuirass and armoured skirt-shaped thigh-protector. (e) Warrior on a relief, kept now in Leiden, encased in a long corselet consisting of metal scales, which are joined with each other by means of leather thongs or metal wire; such a body-armour had no lining, but was worn over some kind of underwear. (f) Personage on a Buddhist relief from Kunduz (Southern Bactria), encased in a cuirass which is reinforced in its upper part by big scale-shaped plates, and in an armoured skirt as well. (g) Armed personage of a stone relief from the Freer Gallery of Art in Washington, who has a quilted corselet of thick soft material as well as armoured skirt as thigh-defence (after Gorelik M V, 1982, pls 4, 6, 8, 9). Worthy of note is the soldiers' method of suspending the sword (b, d, e, g) - by means of a strap passing through the scabbard-slide (see Figs 34q and 44l), which must have been brought to the lands under review by the Kushan conquerors.

Figure 43: (a-c) Engraved plates of bone or horn, which seem to have been the superposed details of a waist-belt, found in Borrow no. 2 of the Orlat cemetery near Samarkand (Sogdia); 1st to 3rd century AD (drawings kindly granted by S A Savchuk; see also the originals photographed in Pugachenkova G A and others, 1991, cat nos 244, 245, 248). All the pieces show enigmatic newcomers who had arrived at Sogdia in the early centuries AD from vast steppe spaces of Central or Inner Asia. (a) Battle scene between two groups of fully armoured warriors both on horseback and on foot, all belonging to one and the same nation. Certainly, a great deal should be said about their armour and weaponry, but here we just want to concentrate on the following: The combatants' tight-fitting headpieces and long armoured coats provided with high collars appear to be like, though not identical, to those in the Khalchayan sculpture (Figs 28c,d and 30a, b,g). Their bows are of the "Sasanian" type (see Fig 44m-o), deserving attention being the *goryti* employed: each of them consists of two sections - a quiver and case, in the latter the bow being in the strung, ready to shoot, position. Another interesting point is in the upper right corner of the scene, where the foot soldier is shown piercing his mounted foe's helmet by a battle-axe of either the *chekan* (Fig 6b-e) or *klevets* (Fig 25c) type. (b) Single combat of unmounted knights, both outfitted in a similar way as above. (c) Hunting scene with riders shooting "Sasanian"-type bows. (d) Representation of the Kushan goddess Nana on a coin of the king Huvishka (second half of the 2nd century), she being shown just releasing an arrow from her long-eared "Sasanian"-type bow (drawing after Gardner P, 1886, pl XXVIII, 7). (e) Bronze medallion depicting the king Huvishka as an elephant-rider armed with a heavy sword (after Göbl R, 1984, pl 176, no 20/l).

Figure 44: (a-l) Weaponry discovered at sites of the Kobadian oasis (in the Lower Kafirnigan valley), in archaeological contexts dating from 4th - 5th century AD (after Sedov A V. *Kobadian na poroge rannego srednevekov'ya*. Moskva, 1987, pl I) - (a) two-edged iron dagger without metal cross-guard and pommel, from the Tulkhar cemetery; (b) two-edged iron dagger with a metal cross-guard, but no metal pommel, from Darakhsha-tepe; (c) polished stone pommel from a sword-or dagger-hilt; (d) single-edged blade from a dagger; (e-k) iron plates from body-armour; (l) fragmentary scabbard-slide of jade (restored, see Fig 34q as well as a detailed study by Trousdale W, 1975). Items (c-l) came from Ak-tepe II. (m) Schematic reconstruction of the "Sasanian"-type bow shown in unstrung (dotted), strung (hatched) and drawn positions (after Brown F E, 1937, fig 3b). (n) Reconstruction of a "Sasanian" bow found at the Karabulak cemetery (in Ferghana), 2nd to 4th century AD (after Moshkova M G, 1992, pl 34,15; not in scale). (o) "Sasanian" bow revealed in 1978 at the Moshchevaya Balka necropolis (in the Northern Caucasus), 8th - 9th century AD; here it is shown in the fighting position, but its string is not depicted. Such bows, 1.2-1.5 m long, with the wooden stave consisting either of one solid piece or of two portions joined together in the handle area, the wooden details being reinforced by sinew, bone and horn laps, were the very powerful range weapons of the Caucasian Alans (after Kaminskii V N, 1982, pp 48-51). (p) Reconstruction of a typical "Hun" bow, usually 1.2-1.6 m long, with horn and bone laps on its handle and ends (after Khazanov A M, 1971, pl XVII,14). (q) Reconstruction of a "Hun"-type bow found at the Kenkol cemetery (in Kirghizstan), first half of 1st millennium AD (after Moshkova M G, 1992, pl 31,22; not in scale). (r-t) Elements of the "severe" curb-bitting, namely (in consecutive order) bronze and iron noseband/muzzles and iron cheeked bit, which were discovered at Susa (South-Western Iran), in deposits dating from 4th century AD (after Ghirshman R in

Studies in Memory of Gaston Wiet, ed. by M Rosen-Ayalon. Jerusalem, 1977, fig 1). (u) Such a combined bitting, shown in operation on the horse of the first Sasanian monarch, Ardashir I, which is represented on the battle relief at Firuzabad (in the province of Fars, Iran); about 230 AD (after Herrmann G in *Archaeologia Iranica et Orientalis*. Vol II, eds. by L De Meyer and E Haerinck. Gent, 1987, p 784, Fig 2a). This new bitting type, invented to improve controlling the horse by more severe pressure upon its tongue, was introduced into Iranian horsemanship, according to pictorial evidence, not later than the early 3rd century AD (see the cited article by G Herrmann, pp 758-763). For the Bactrian region proper, this device is well visible on Fig 47b,d (see also Pl 8D).

Figure 45: (a) Terracotta slab from Dal'verzin-tepe, with the image of an armed goddess sitting on a tiger-like animal; 3rd - 4th century AD. The personage wears a helmet with four-cornered brim, waist-length cuirass, "hooped" arm-protector encasing her right arm, belt and armoured (?) skirt; her weapon is a trident (drawing after Pougatchenkova G A *Les Trésors de Dalverzine-tépé*. Leningrad, 1978, figs 52 and 53; about its date and interpretation see the same author's article in *Vestnik Drevnei Istorii* 1989, no 4, pp 96-105). (b, c) Wall-painting fragments from Dil'berjin, depicting female divinities who have helmets going back to the "Boeotian" those; 3rd to 4th century AD (drawings after Kruglikova I T, in *Comptes rendus des séances de l'Académie des inscriptions et belles-lettres* 1977, figs 11 and 12). (d) Warrior pictured on a silver bowl, which was found at the Kustanai district (in Kazakhstan) in 1903 (now in the Hermitage, Sankt-Petersburg); the bowl belongs to the so-called "Bactrian" silver vessels with late "hellenized" ornaments in relief and dates from the time around 400 AD. The personage under review is dressed in a helmet similar to those just mentioned, as well as "muscle" cuirass (drawing after Trever K V, 1940, pl 17

below; about the date see Marshak B I in *Antichnost' i antichnye traditsii v kul'ture i iskusstve narodov Sovetskogo Vostoka*, ed. by I R Bichikyan. Moskva, 1978, p 259). True, it remains uncertain whether these headpieces (and, incidentally, those on Fig 39a,b as well) originating from Hellenistic armament tradition were in actual use at so late a time, or their representations were due only to the borrowing of much earlier pictorial models.

Figure 46: Horsemen represented in lion-hunting scenes of a silver "Bactrian"-style bowl, which was revealed at Vereino (in the Perm region) in 1872 (now in the Hermitage collection); 4th - 5th century AD (drawings after Trever K V, 1940, pls 22-24). See Pl 8B,C as reconstructions.

Figure 47: (a) Chionitan/Kidarite (?) gem-seal, kept in the Hermitage, with a male portrait and one-word cursive inscription in Bactrian; about mid-4th century AD (after Staviskii B Ya in *Soobshcheniya Gosudarstvennogo Ermitazha* XX, 1961, fig at p 56, left). The inscription runs: ACBAPOBIDO, that is "chief of cavalry" (Henning W B in *Bulletin of the School of Oriental and African Studies* XXV, 1962, pt 2, p 335). Therefore, it is a title of the seal-owner, whose image is shown here. (b-d) Riders represented on the so-called "Hephthalite" silver bowl with hunting scenes, from the British Museum; 5th century AD (drawings after Bivar A D H, 1972, figs 20-22; there, at p 282, the bowl is called "Kidarite", but compare our explanation concerning an ethnic attribution to Pl 8D dealing with a summarized reconstruction of these mounted warriors.

COLOUR PLATE DESCRIPTIONS

Plate 1 - Bactrian warriors under the Achaemenids (400 to 330 BC)

(1A)   Armed priest
(1B)   Light infantryman
(1C)   Mounted nobleman in hunting outfit
(1D)   Heavily armed infantryman

This plate depicts Bactrian soldiery reconstructed after depictions on the Oxus Treasure works of art. Figure (1A) is a priest (*magus*) of the Zoroastrian faith based on our Fig 4a. He stands on a hill before the fire altar (which is shown on a much later Sasanian coin) and performs some cult rite with a special ceremonial bunch of wooden rods (*barsom*) in his right hand, anticipating the beginning of either a battle action or taking the field. He wears typical "Median" dress (a knee-length belted tunic, tight-fitting trousers and hood-like cap) and has a short sword (*acinaces*) suspended from his right side. Similarly equipped is the warrior (1B) based on Fig 4b, but he is additionally armed with a spear provided with a small ball-shaped butt of bronze; his *acinaces*-sheath corresponds to that from Takht-i Sangin (Fig 5b).

The cavalryman (1C) is based on noble hunters on the silver disc (Fig 3a-c). He is shown wearing a "mounted" version of the "Median" dress, namely a short, waist-length tunic (see also Fig 4d,e), here decorated by a vertical central strip with a row of precious stones. His weaponry consists of a short spear, employed for both casting at a distance and striking in close combat, as well as a small "Scythian"-type bow in a quiver. His horse's mane is clipped to facilitate mounted bow use, and its twisted tail is tied up with a band. Note the richly ornamented and crenellated saddle-cloth.

The infantryman (1D), who is based on the only representation, for the period under review, of a Bactrian warrior encased in full armour (Fig 4c), is dressed in the following outfit: a bronze tight-fitting helmet going back probably to the "Kuban"-type head-defences (see Fig 6a) and crowned with a long feathered plume; a waist-length corselet of plain leather, reinforced with two bronze lapels to protect both the chest and shoulders; a thigh-protector in the shape of a skirt consisting of leather or thick fabric narrow strips (Greek *pteryges*); arm-guards in the shape of flexible tubes composed of narrow hoop-like pieces made of leather rather than metal. As his offensive weapons the personage has a pick-like battle axe-*chekan* with straight iron blade (see Fig 6d) and wooden handle, spear and the well-known Scythian/Saca combined bowcase-quiver (Greek *gorytos*) to hold both the bow and the arrows.

Plate 2 - Graeco-Bactrian war-elephant and three-man Crew (late 3rd century BC)

(2A)   War-elephant and its equipment
(2B)   Mahout
(2C)   Heavily armed soldier of Greek origin
(2D)   Lightly armed young Bactrian

The war-elephant and its personnel consisting of a driver and two warriors are tentatively reconstructed here after depictions on the two silver *phalerae* of Graeco-Bactrian workmanship, kept now in the Hermitage in Sankt-Petersburg (Fig 16a,b). The animal (2A) is of the Indian type; it carries a crenellated tower made of wooden planks, the outside surface of which is decorated with the shapes of arrows and crosses (possibly made of metal plates). The tower contains javelins to be used for casting from above in combat; its foundation, shaped to fit the elephant's back, stands on a saddle-cloth which is embroidered with a dragon. The tower is fastened to the animal's body by a broad girth-strap passing through the saddle-cloth and by iron breast- and crupper chains. The mahout (2B), perhaps of Indian origin, wears only light garments. His tool for driving the elephant is an iron crook (*ank*) known also from actual finds (Fig 14c-e).

On the *phalerae* only the head of the soldier of the tower crew (2C), is seen, wearing a Greek "Boeotian"-type helmet. He is shown by us as a fighter in full Greek panoply which includes, besides the helmet, a bronze "muscle"-type cuirass, *pteryges*-type thigh-protector and bronze greaves (*knemides*). He is armed with a spear and short straight sword (*xiphos*). Also just shown here hypothetically is the second tower warrior as a young, beardless Bactrian (2D), whose head, wearing neither cap nor helmet, is visible on the *phalerae*. He is dressed in light garments of the "Median" style and his weapons go back to the Achaemenid epoch.

Plate 3 - Graeco-Bactrian and Indo-Greek troop and command types under King Eucratides the Great (170 - 145 BC)

(3A)   Armoured foot soldier of the *thyreophoros* type
(3B)   Heavy lancer (*sarissophorus*) of Eucratides' mounted bodyguard
(3C)   King's foot bodyguard
(3D)   Indo-Greek general on horseback

This plate deals with warrior types acting in the time of the mighty king Eucratides the Great, who reigned not only over Bactria but also over some territories to the south of the Hindukush. The foot solder (3A) based on the terracotta plaque from Kampyr-tepe (Fig 24a) is shown wearing a spiked helmet of bronze, plain (not "muscle") cuirass of iron provided with a stand-up collar, thigh-protector of the *pteryges* type and bronze greaves-*knemides*. He carries a short Greek sword with iron blade of stretched rhomboid form (*xiphos*).

His large oval shield goes back, most likely, to the typical Celtic *thyreos*, though such a distinctive feature of the latter as a spindle-shaped boss is replaced here by a massive emblem of metal in relief, which possibly depicts a lizard; this emblem has perhaps not only a decorative function but also a strengthening one like the spindle-shaped boss of the *thyreos*.

The cavalryman (3B) is reconstructed after depictions on Eucratides' coins which show on the reverse the heavenly twins Dioscuri charging with very long lances-*sarissae* (Fig 19b). The Dioscuri were usually represented in Hellenistic and Roman art as nude men, without any body-armour. In reality such mounted lancers, whose function was to fight in close combat, had to wear corselets, so our rider has a Greek "muscle" cuirass well adapted to cavalry usage. Besides that, he also wears a bronze conical helmet of the "Pilos" type, which was peculiar to the Dioscuri iconography of Eucratides' coins (see Fig 8g), and *pteryges*-type thigh-protector. His *sarissa*, about 4.5m long, is provided with an iron butt-spike (here after Fig 8b, but compare 8k,l). It seems quite possible that the Dioscuri on the coins of Eucratides copy, to some extent, horsemen of the king's bodyguard picked regiment, 300 in number, as described by Justinus (XLI,6,4). Although the palm on his back and the star on his helmet are very unlikely, if not impossible, for an actual warrior, as opposed to one of the heavenly twins, we have decided still to portray them in our reconstruction.

The foot bodyguard (3C) is based upon the two gold clasps from Grave no 3 of the Tillya-tepe necropolis (Fig 24e,f). Although this burial is dated itself to the first half of the 1st century AD, the pieces under review seem to be of much earlier date. Most probably, they were manufactured by a local master, either in the Late Graeco-Bactrian or in the very Early Yüeh-chih period, that is within the second half of the 2nd century BC. In any case, most of our warrior's outfit, particularly a helmet of the "sharp forehead peak" type, elaborately produced "muscle" cuirass and short sword with a hilt shaped into the griffin's head, are of obvious Hellenistic origin. Deserving attention is the method of suspending the sword - by means of the scabbard-slide. Assuming our dating is correct, then we are witnessing the earliest use of the scabbard-slide in the Bactrian region. Taking into account the parade aspects of both the warriors on the clasps, it seems acceptable to depict the whole armour assemblage on our reconstruction as made of gilt metal.

The mounted general (3D) is based upon coin representations of the Indo-Greek ruler Antimachus II Nicephorus (Fig 19d). He wears a broad-brimmed hat of cloth or felt, probably the Graeco-Macedonian *petasos*. His armour consists of a "muscle" cuirass of bronze, added here hypothetically, and thigh-protector of the *pteryges* type. Worthy of note is his horse's long saddle-cloth with the lower edge decorated with a crenellated ornament. On the whole, this figure's outfit is rather for the march than the battle.

Plate 4 - Yüeh-chih combined cavalry force at the very beginning of 1st century AD

(4A-B) Lightly armed horse-archers
(4C) Heavily outfitted cavalryman-
         cataphractarius

Reconstructions of the mounted archers are based on the ivory casket panel from Takht-i Sangin (4A, see Fig 27a) and on the sculptural fragments from Khalchayan (4B, see Fig 29; compare 31a as well). The warrior (4A), dressed in a long caftan, has a compound bow with long stiffened ears, which belongs to the so-called "Sasanian" type (see Fig 44m-o), a long sheathed sword and quiver, both suspended from his waist-belt.

The bowman (4B), wearing a long belted shirt, carries a long, double arched compound bow of the so-called "Hun" type

(see Fig 44p), which is shown here speculatively, being a weapon that could have been brought to Bactria by the Yüeh-chih tribal coalition from the Central Asian steppes, where such bows must have already been in use. A bow of this type, dating from the first half of 1st millennium AD, was found in a catacomb burial of the Kenkol cemetery in Kirghizstan (see Fig 44q). The unique saddle with a rigid framework (perhaps made of wood), is known in the period under review solely thanks to the Khalchayan sculptural piece (see Fig 29h). Note the differences between the bowmen's hair-styles, which may indicate various Yüeh-chih tribes or clans. The painted sculpture from Khalchayan suggests that clothes were typically made of white cotton and red wool, although one figure, a ruler, wears what might be called "aquamarine".

The *cataphractarius* (4C) is based on the sculptural fragments from Khalchayan (Fig 30), our reconstruction differing from an earlier one by G A Pugachenkova (Fig 31a,b) in some important details, such as the warrior's leg-guards and his horse's armoured trapper. The rider's long corselet and arm-guards are here identical in their constructions with those depicted on the Indo-Saca coins (Fig 26a,c,d). As to his head-protector, it seems to be of the so-called "ridge" style, provided with a low fore-and-aft crest or ridge piece, as well as with a forehead peak and cheek-pieces. The leg-guards, reconstructed after a very small fragment (Fig 30e), consist of two parts. The upper one is a short "tube" of iron hoops encasing the lower portion of the thigh and reaching the knee (note that the Khalchayan armoured coat is slightly shorter than the Indo-Saca one and therefore it does not cover the whole thigh). The other part consists of trousers armoured by vertical strips of iron scales, however, the central strip is different, namely being of dark leather; it is reinforced by very small, tick-shaped iron plaques forming a herringbone design. It goes without saying that this reconstruction is very tentative. The horse-armour, as depicted in the sculpture (Fig 30c,d), comprises three items: a head-mask of armoured bronze scales; a neck-defence (Greek *peritrakhelion*) composed of a fabric or leather lining armoured by vertical rows of big bronze scales provided with longitudinal ribs for hardness; an armoured trapper which, in our speculative reconstruction, is of the same construction as the neck-defence; they both are fastened together by means of leather laces. As regards the horseman's offensive weapons, missing from the sculpture, they were hardly likely to be different from the standard cataphract heavy *contus* and long sword.

Plate 5 - Bactrian nobles under Kanishka I the Great (first half of 2nd century AD)

(5A)   King Kanishka the Great
(5B)   Kushano-Bactrian noble in everyday dress
(5C)   Kushano-Bactrian noble warrior on foot

The figure of Kanishka (5A) is mainly based on his statue from Mathura (Fig 38e). His headgear has been restored after some of his coins (Fig 41d). The king is shown wearing a long beltless caftan over a long belted undergarment. He holds two weapons as badges of power. His heavy mace or club is made of wooden pieces held together by gilt metal hoops; its top is decorated with a gilt metal head of an Indian *makara*, a crocodilian monster. His left hand grips the hilt of his massive sheathed sword, the hilt being shaped into a bird's head and neck. The richly ornamented scabbard is attached not to a waist-belt, as usual, but to the over-caftan itself, using two points of fastening; firstly, by means of a leather strap passing through the scabbard-slide, and secondly, by another strap fastened to the scabbard rear slightly above the scabbard-slide.

The personage (5B) is based on representations from Kampyr-tepe, above all on a silver statuette (Fig 36d,e). He may be interpreted as a chief of this fortress garrison, dressed in everyday garments. They are typical for Yüeh-chih and Kushan Bactria (see also Figs 31h and 36b) and consist of a long-sleeved caftan below the waist, wrapped over to the left and belted, and wide trousers (*sharovary*).

The noble warrior (5C) is based on terracotta figurines from Kampyre-tepe and the Termez Museum (Fig 36c,f), on which each of the personages is encased in a "muscle" cuirass, broad protective belt set in a metal frame and armoured skirt. They also have shields which are positioned by their left legs, but only the edges of which can be seen. Hence, the warrior's round shield with knobbly decoration, shown in our reconstruction, is of a type known from Great Kushan coins (Fig 40a). The long double-edged sword, hypothetically added here, is the same as those of Yüeh-chih/Kushan soldiery, found in Bactria (Fig 33a,b). Note that the reconstruction of the armoured skirt presented here is speculative; it could take a different form, for example like that of our (3C).

Plate 6 - Martial parade equipment of the Later Great Kushan Kings (late 2nd to first quarter of 3rd century AD)

(6A)   Kanishka II (late 2nd century)
(6B-D) Vasudeva - three variants
          (first quarter of 3rd century),

All the reconstructions are based upon the royal portrayals on coins (Figs 39c and 40a-c). The personages wear conical helmets probably of the so-called "spangenhelm"-type, which are thought to be a metal interpretation of the felt caps of the steppe nomads. They were constructed of a framework of iron or bronze straps, into which metal plates were fitted. The helmets of the figures (6A, 6C, 6D) are richly decorated with symbols laid on their surface, while the framework construction of the helmet (6B) is entirely covered by scale armour. In two cases (6A, 6C) there are aventails. The arms and legs of the kings are equally encased in hooped tube-like defences. M V Gorelik (1982, p.85) has expressed an alternative opinion that the leg-defences, depicted on the Kushan coins, were in reality not tubes, but pieces of soft material armoured by metal half-hoops. Indeed, proceeding from some vague pictures on coins, the application of such leg-armour by the Kushans seems to be quite permissible. However, this does not invalidate the "tube theory". As to corselets, three of them (6A-6C) are long armoured coats, whereas the fourth one (6D) is shorter and waist-length; an armoured skirt protects the thighs. Presumably, all the royal armour items represented would have been made of iron or bronze and gilded with gold pellicles.

The kings' weapons are tridents and long swords, the former probably a badge of royal power rather than a real fighting arm. Three methods of suspending swords are shown: Firstly, by means of a scabbard-slide (6A, 6B); secondly, by means of a metal frame-like device attached both to the scabbard and, by a leather strap, to the waist-belt (6D), and thirdly, the scabbard is attached directly to the waist-belt (6C).

Plate 7 - Gandharan warriors

(7A-D) Armoured foot soldiers
(7E-F) Female palace guards

This plate shows foot warriors of the North-Western Indian region in the great Kushan epoch, as depicted in the famous sculptural art of Gandhara.

Much of the armour and equipment of Gandhara seems to have been inspired by the Yüeh-chih/Kushan newcomers, who in turn had adopted much of it in the Central Asian regions, including Bactria. For examples see our Fig. 42c-f. Also especially illustrative are the materials adduced by M V Gorelik in his paper on Kushan armour (Gorelik M. V., 1982, pls 4-12). For further examples see any or all of:

Hallade M. *The Gandhara Style-and the evolution of Buddhist Art*. London, 1968.
Joshi N P and Sharma RC. *Catalogue of Gandhara Sculptures in the State Museum, Lucknow*. Lucknow, 1969.
Marshall Sir John. *The Buddhist Art of Gandhara* ...Cambridge, 1960.
Nehru L. *Origins of the Gandharan Style* ... Delhi, 1989.

Many Gandharan works of art of the period under consideration show scenes from the life of Buddha, including his flight from the royal palace (whence the female guards in our picture are derived) and his confrontation with the forces of the evil Mara, which have provided some of the details on our foot warriors, in particular the shield decorated with a monstrous face (7D). The accusation might therefore be levelled that this is really only a 'fantasy' shield but it is highly probable that such devices could still adorn the shields of actual warriors.

Plate 8 - Warriors in Bactria-Tokharistan in the Late Kushan Period

(8A-B) Kidarite Huns (or Chionitae) in
        hunting dress (about 400 AD)
(8C)   Hephthalite cavalryman (about 450)

The horsemen (8A and 8B), speculatively supposed by us as the alien Chionitae-Kidaritai, are based upon depictions on the silver bowl from the Hermitage collection (Fig 46a-c), where they are shown in hunting action. Being lightly armed, they carry double-arched compound bows of the "Sasanian" type as well as cylindrical quivers attached to the saddle-cloth, inside of which both arrows and a soft leather bowcase (for keeping the unstrung bow) are contained. The riders also have massive swords suspended at their waist-belts and, in one case (8B), a heavy lance. In times much earlier than the period this plate depicts it would appear, from evidence from painted plaster, that clothes (of probably both the Yüeh-chih and the Kushans) were predominantly white and red, perhaps excepting those for the very rich or powerful, but during this later period we have allowed a greater latitude of choice (or we might assume these two are particularly affluent hunters).

The warrior (8C) is supposedly a Hephthalite conqueror of Tokharistan. He is reconstructed after depictions on a silver bowl in the British Museum (Fig 47b-d). His weaponry includes a "Sasanian-type" bow, quiver and long massive sword suspended to his waist-belt by means of the scabbard-slide. This warrior may be identified as a Hephthalite by origin because of his "pointed" head, shown in the original source without any headgear (Fig 47c). The shape of the head was due to an artificial circular deformation of the skull, which, as Ch. de Ujfalvy has demonstrated (in *L'Anthropologie* IX, 1898, pp.395-397) is a characteristic feature of the coin portraits of the Hephthalite rulers of Northern India. Especially deserving attention here is the horse's metal bit system consisting of a noseband/muzzle and a bit provided on each side of the mouth with a curved cheekpiece. Actual finds of the pieces from such a bit system, intended for more severe control of the horse were found in 4th century AD levels at Susa (South-Western Iran). See also Fig 44r-t, as well as 44u, from 3rd century Sasanian sources.

FRONTISPIECE (Black & white) - Nomadic Conquerors and Lords of Bactria (1st century BC to mid-1st century AD).

(LEFT)   Indo-Saca/Scythian ruler Spalirises (first quarter of 1st century BC)
(RIGHT) Early Kushan sovereign of Bactria (about mid-1st century AD)

This picture shows reconstructions of high-rank warriors of steppe origin, as they are depicted in the iconography of nomadic chieftains ruling over Bactria and neighbouring lands after the Greeks. Although the most likely dates of the two figures concerned are not identical we have allowed a little artistic licence, for slightly older fashions could have lingered on into slightly later periods. The heavily armed cavalryman-*cataphractarius* (LEFT) is based on the coin of Spalirises (Fig 26a), king of the so-called Indo-Saca state. He is pictured on the coin without a metal helmet, usual on coins of other Indo-Saca kings (Fig 26c), but in a typical nomadic cap, belonging to the *bashlyk* type. He wears a very long armoured coat composed of a cloth or leather lining with big square plates of iron, and with an iron annular collar; it has deep slits at the front and rear to facilitate use on horseback. His arms are encased in tube-like defences. His weapon is the standard cataphract's heavy lance, about 3.0-3.5m long.

The Early Kushan sovereign of Bactria (RIGHT) is reconstructed on the basis of the coins issued by a ruler denominating himself "King of Kings, Great Saviour" (Fig 37d), who is sometimes thought to have been the first Great Kushan emperor, Kujula Kadphises. He is shown here wearing a "two-horned" hat (*tiara*) and short, waist-length corselet of iron scales over a long caftan (true, the presence of the body-armour is speculative on the grounds of some vague signs on the coins). The personage holds in his right hand a battle-axe with a curved pointed blade (*klevets*), a badge of royal power rather than a fighting weapon (see also Figs 25c and 26b).

Plate 1 - Bactrian warriors under the Achaemenids (400 to 330 BC)

Plate 2 - Graeco-Bactrian war-elephant and three-man crew (late 3rd century BC)

(3A)

(3B)

(3C)

(3D)

Plate 3 - Graeco-Bactrian and Indo-Greek troop and command types under King Eucratides the Great (170 - 145 BC)

Plate 4 - Yüeh-chih combined cavalry force at the very beginning of 1st century AD

(4A)

(4B)

(5C)

(5A)

(5B)

Plate 5 - Bactrian nobles under Kanishka I the Great (first half of 2nd century AD)

Plate 6 - Martial parade equipment of the Later Great Kushan Kings (late 2nd to first quarter of 3rd century AD)

Plate 7 - Gandharan warriors

Plate 8 - Warriors in Bactria-Tokharistan in the Late Kushan period

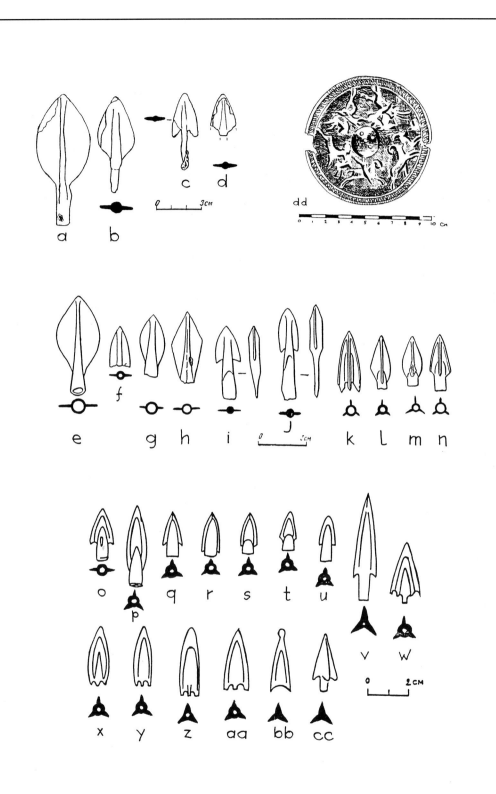

Figure 1.

33

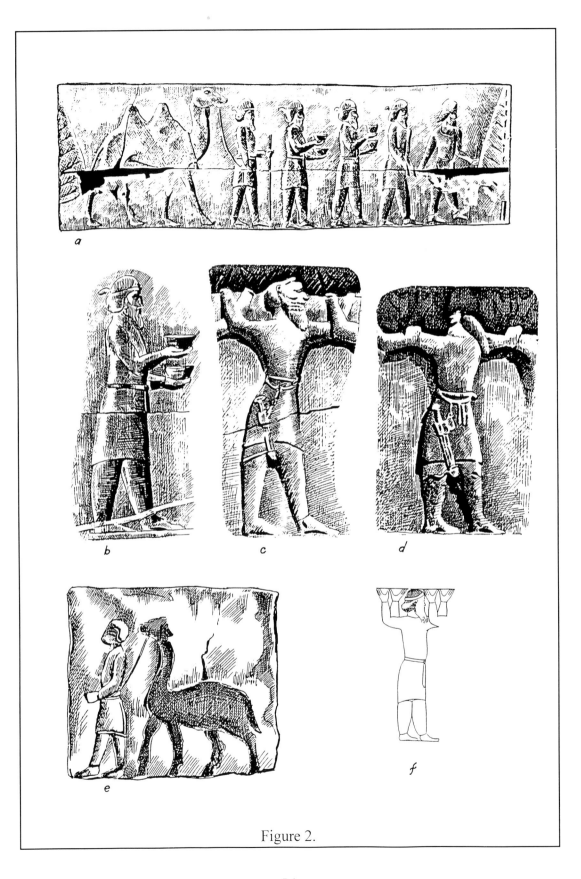

Figure 2.

34

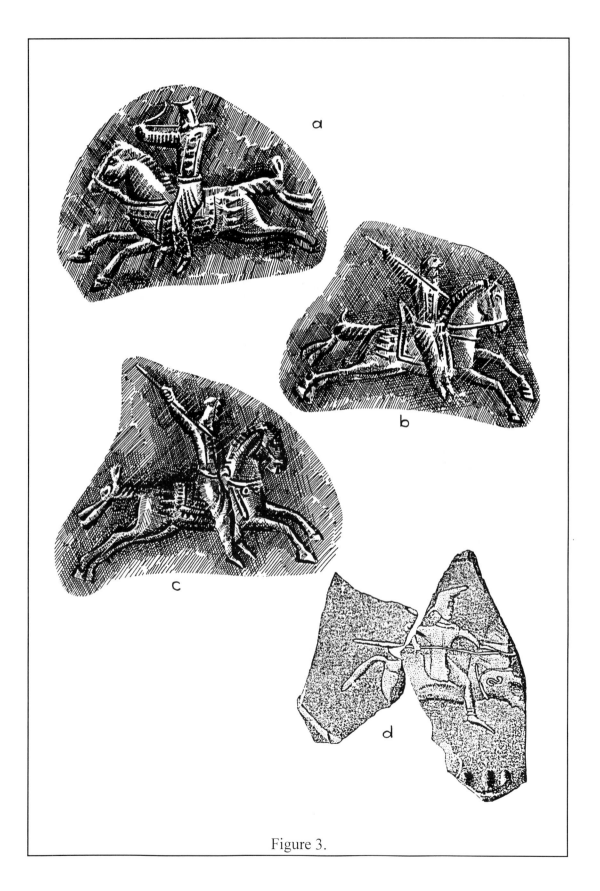

Figure 3.

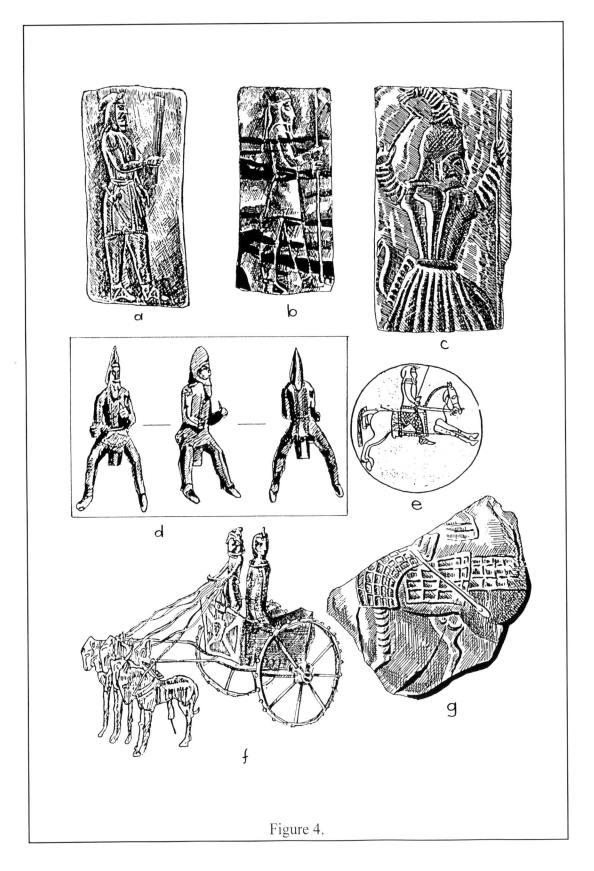

Figure 4.

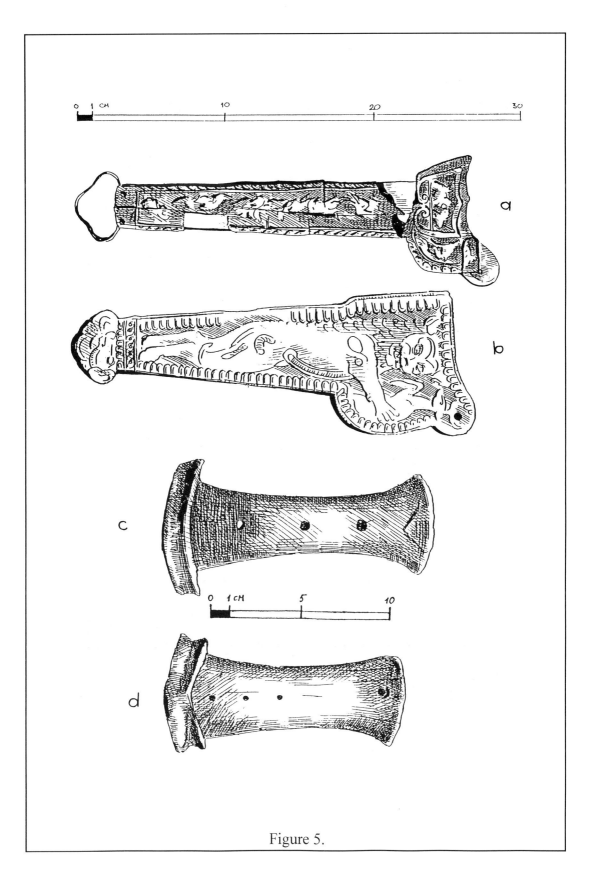

Figure 5.

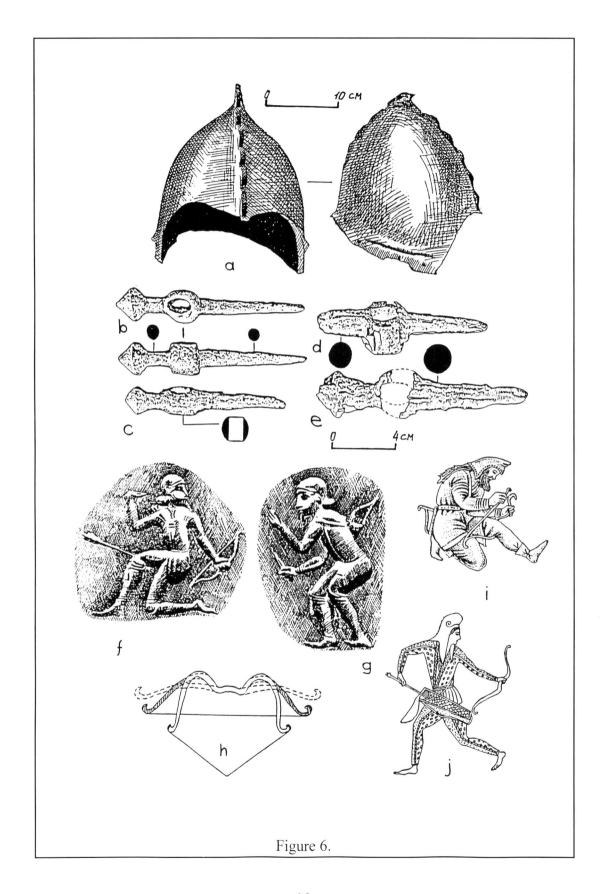

Figure 6.

Figure 7.

39

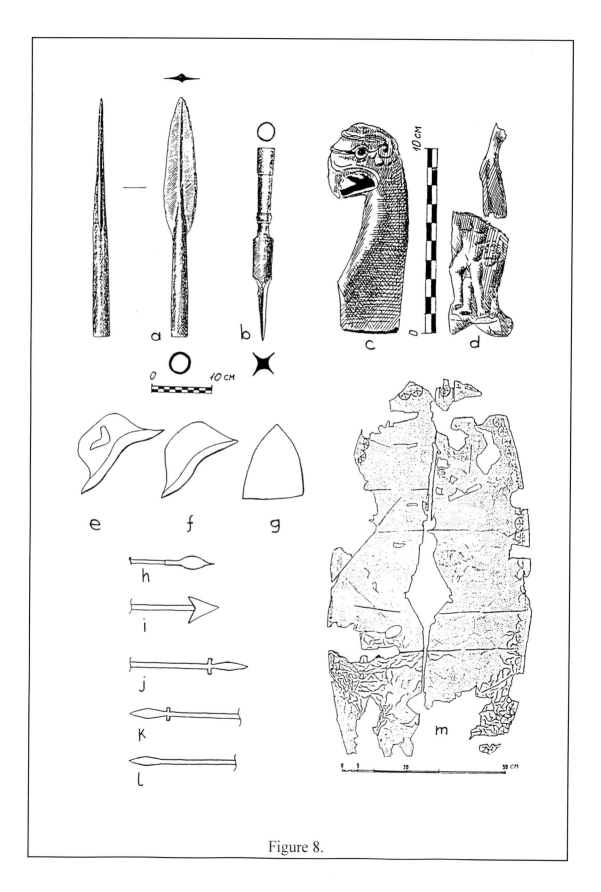

Figure 8.

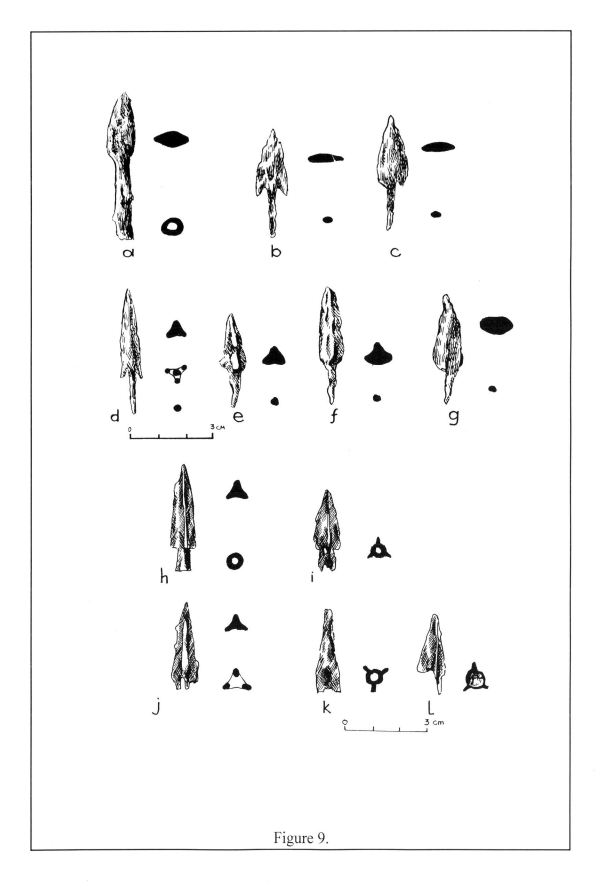

Figure 9.

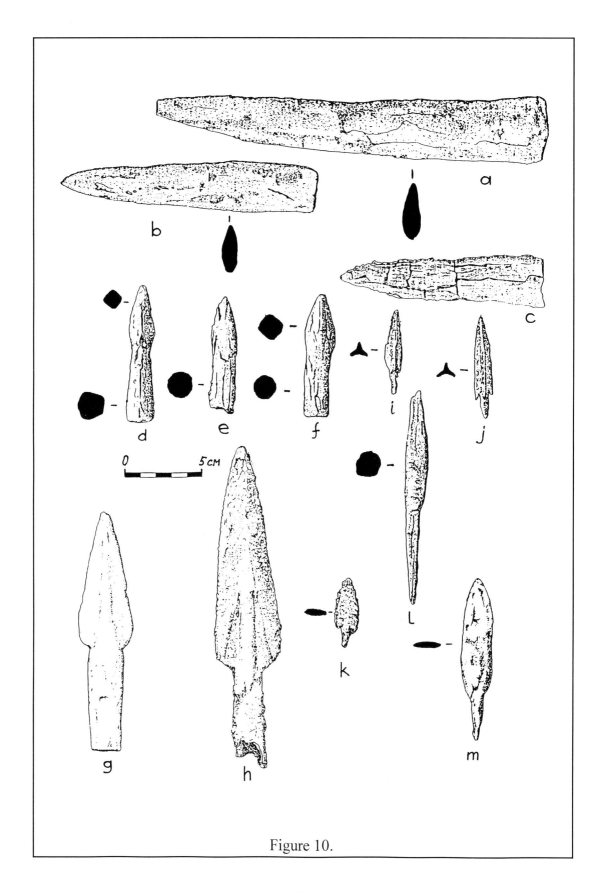

Figure 10.

42

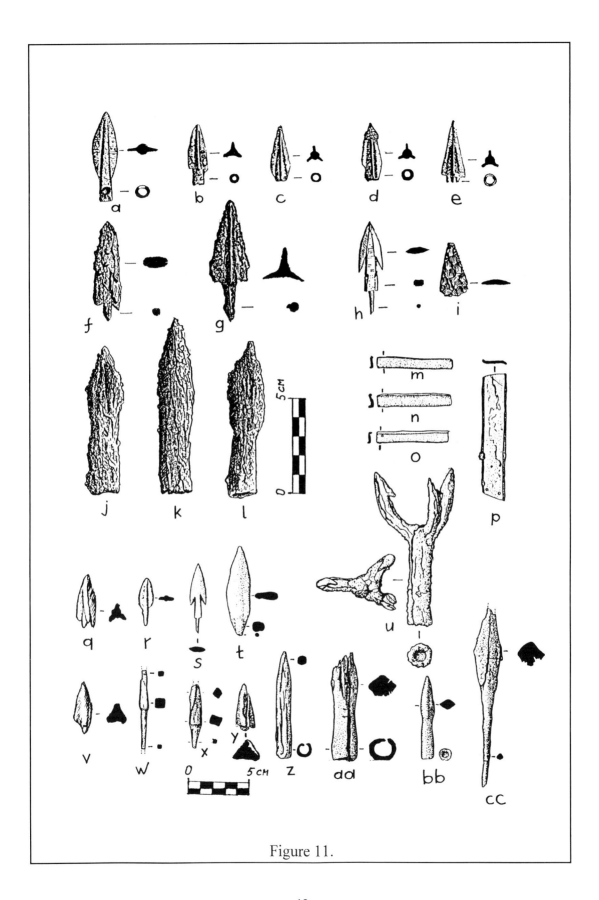

Figure 11.

43

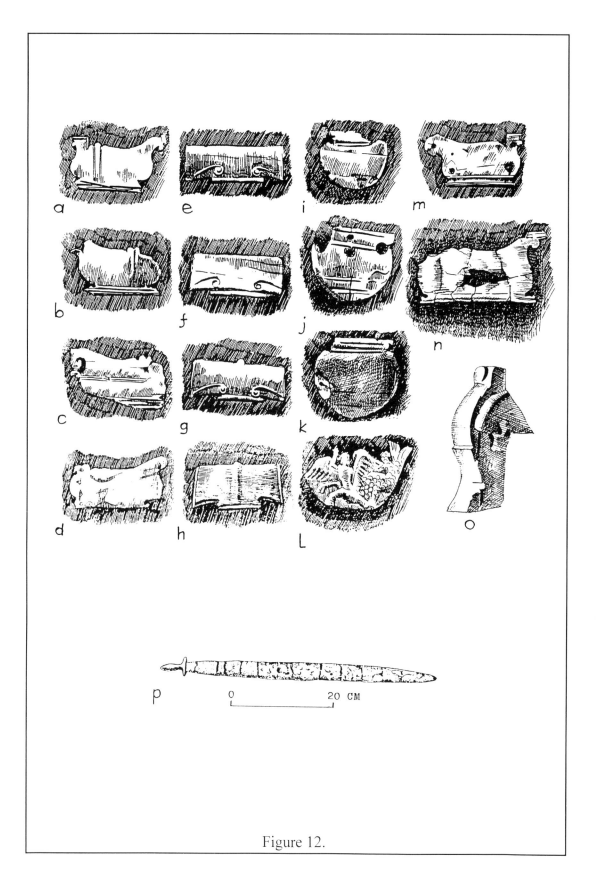

Figure 12.

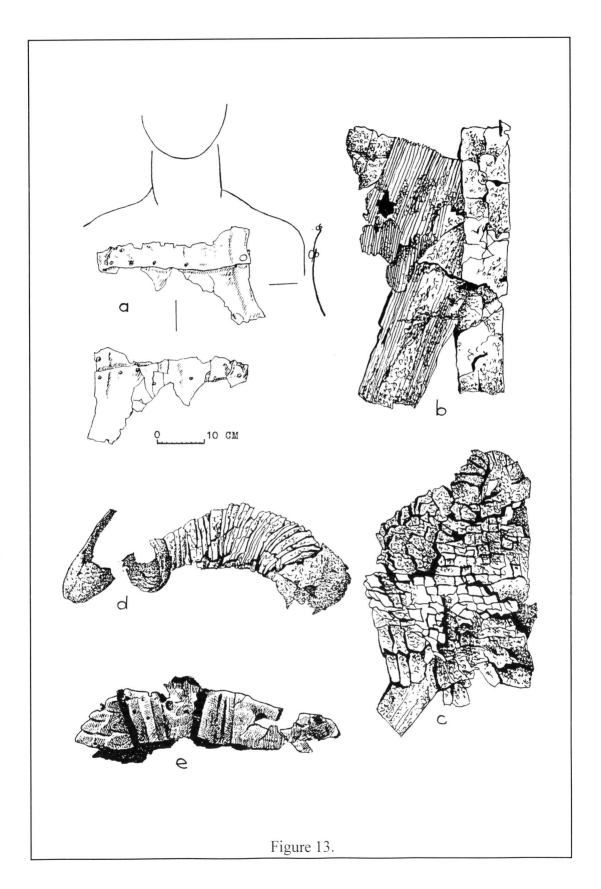

Figure 13.

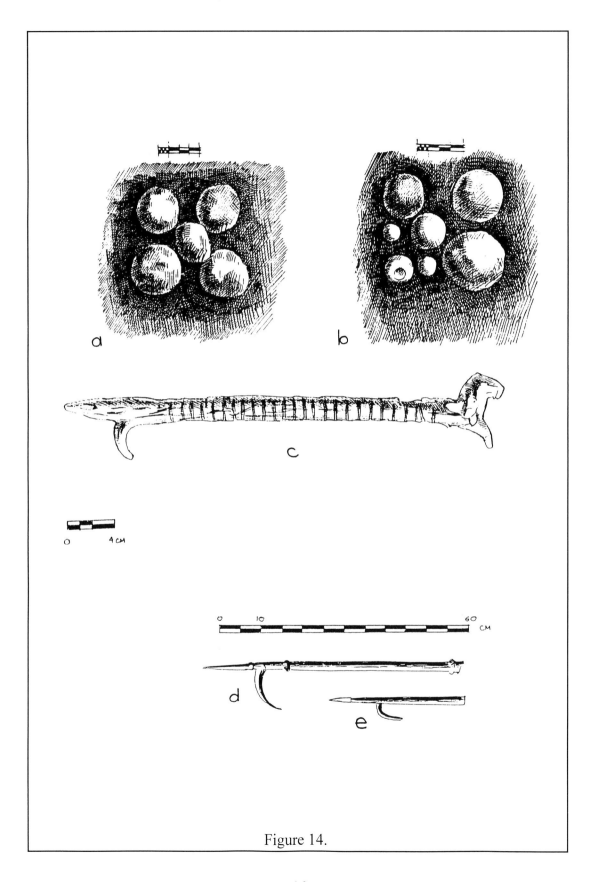

Figure 14.

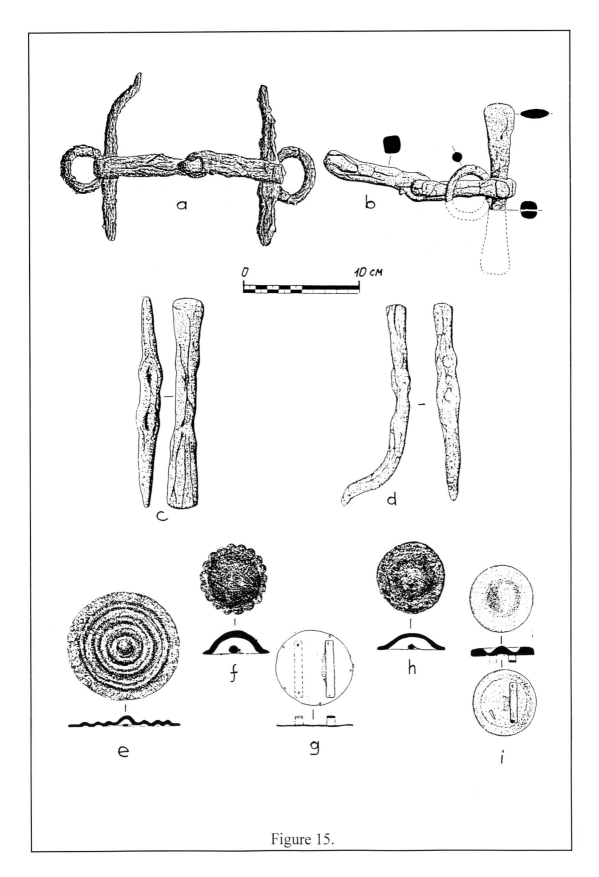

0   10 CM

Figure 15.

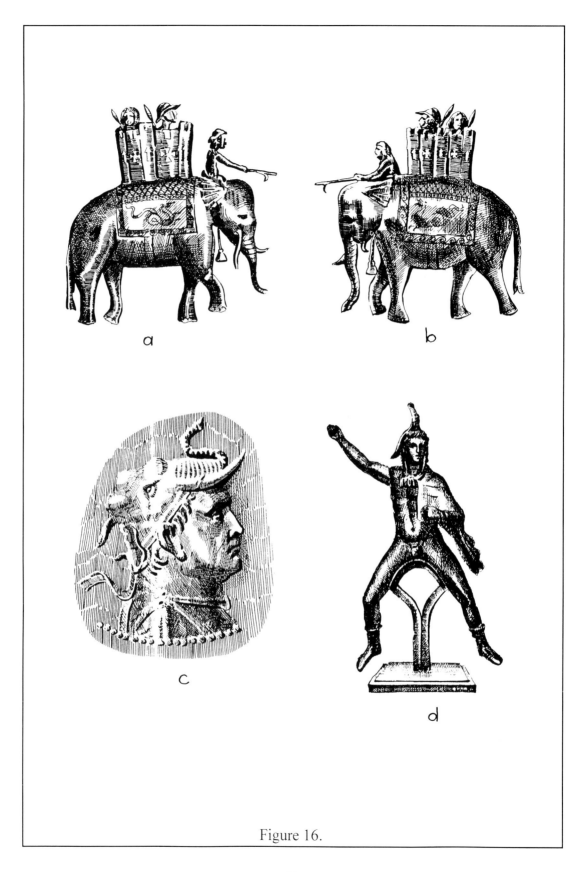

a

b

c

d

Figure 16.

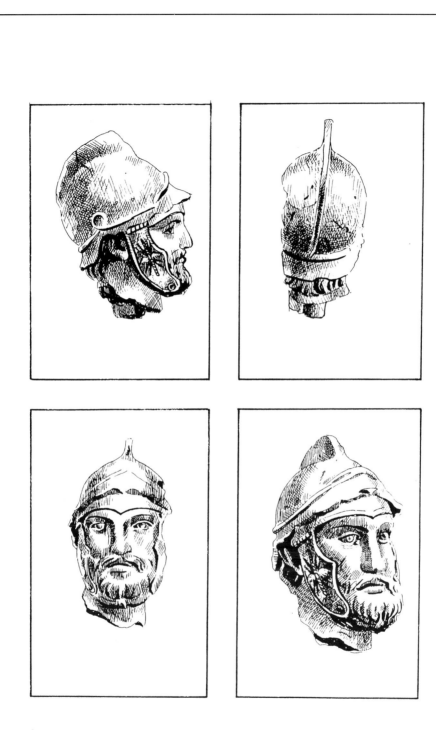

Figure 17.

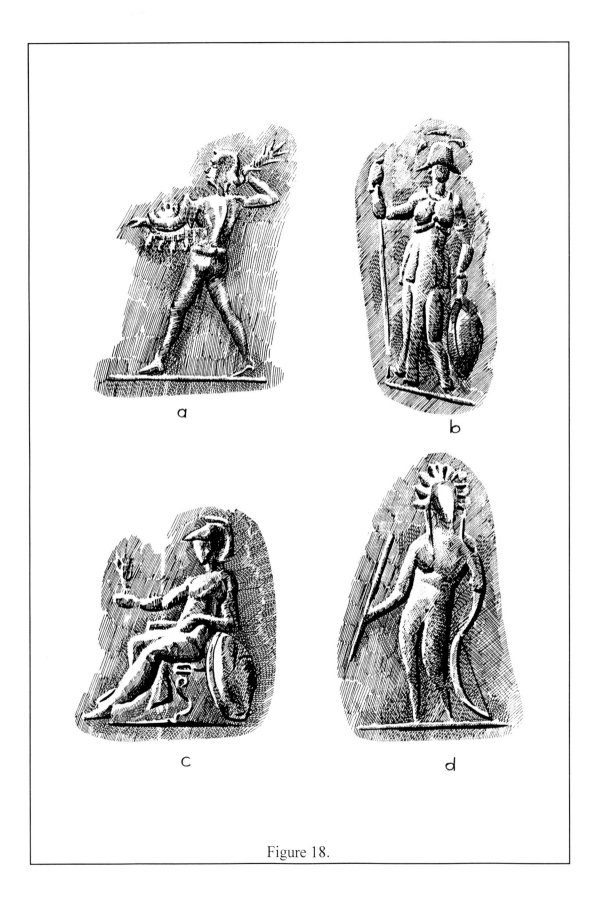

Figure 18.

Figure 19.

Figure 20.

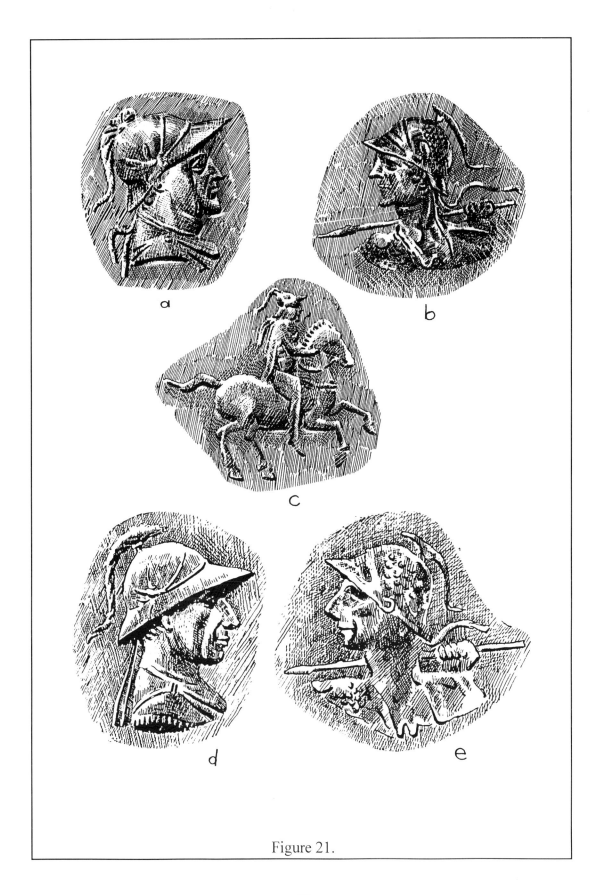

Figure 21.

53

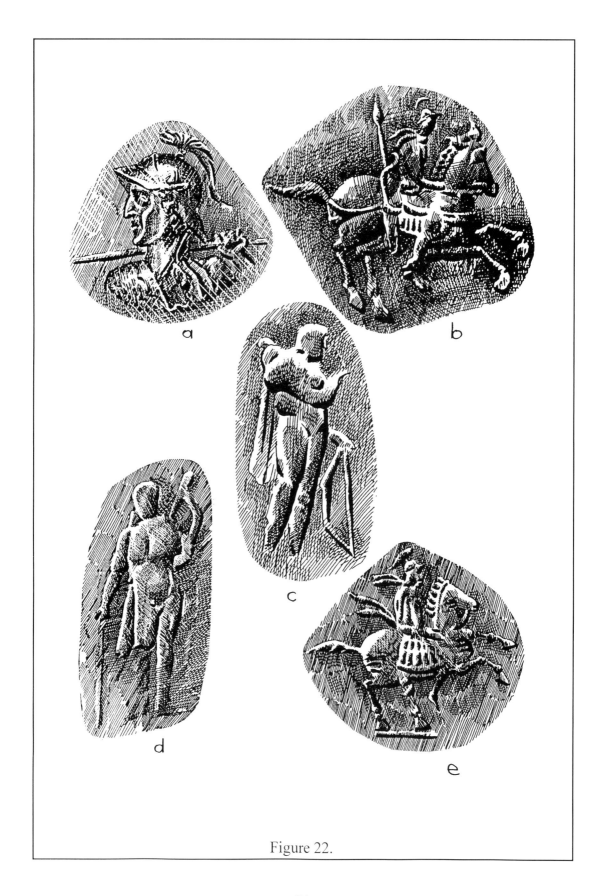

Figure 22.

54

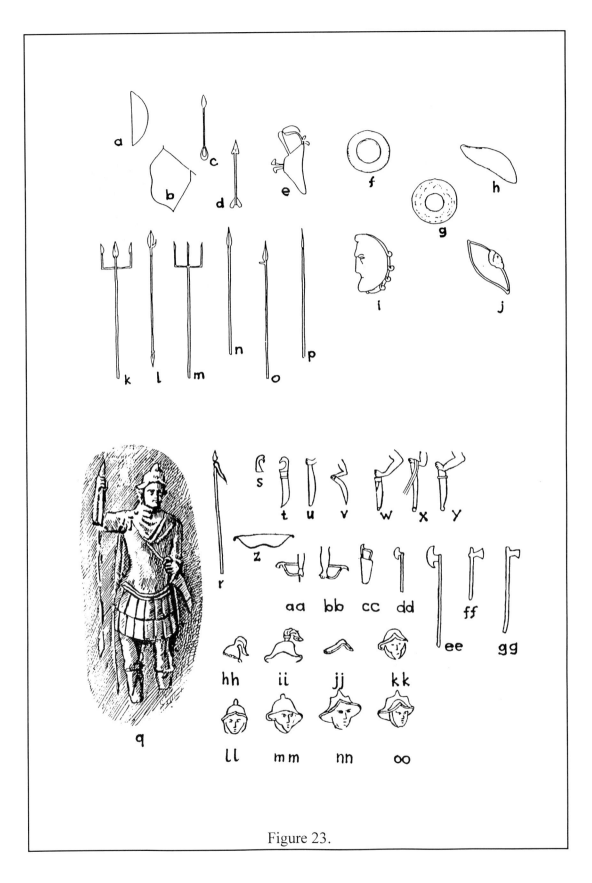

Figure 23.

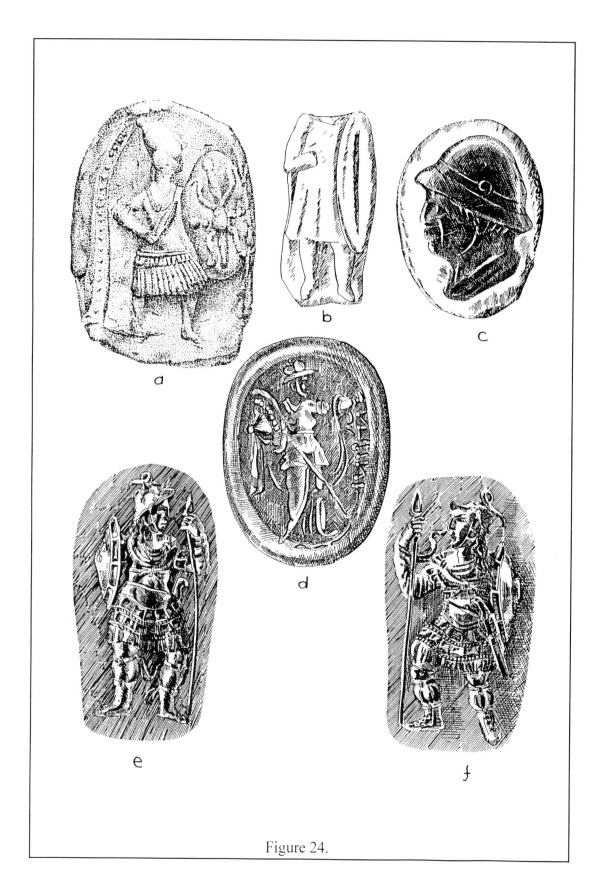

Figure 24.

56

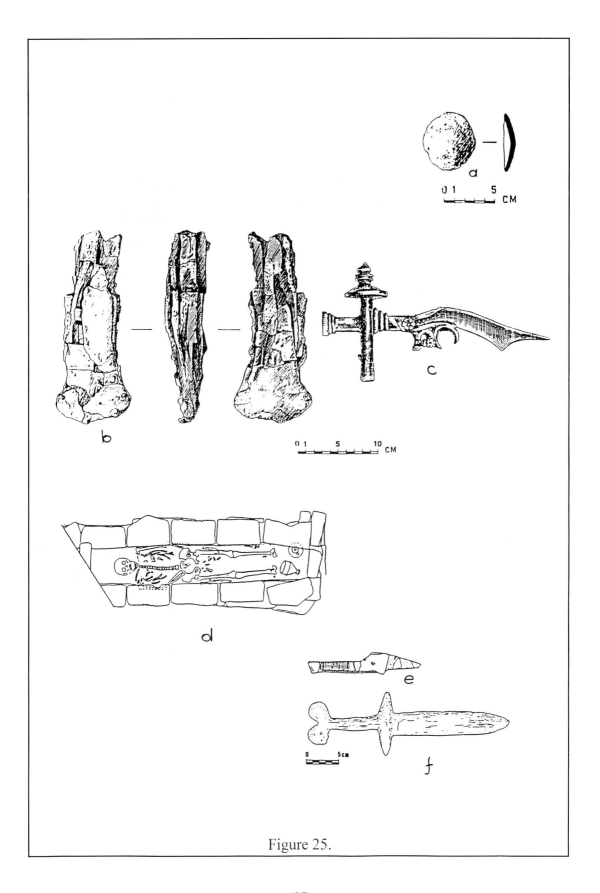

Figure 25.

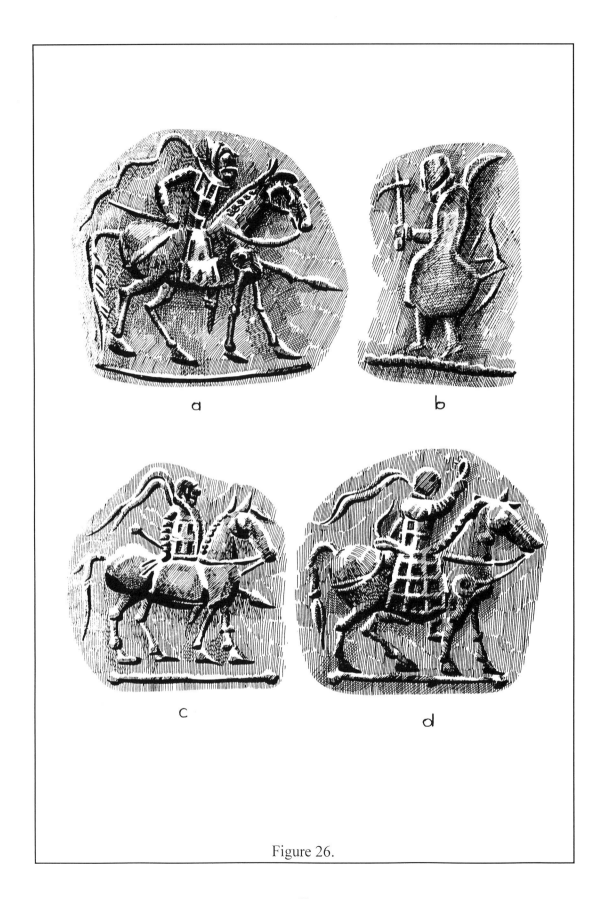

Figure 26.

58

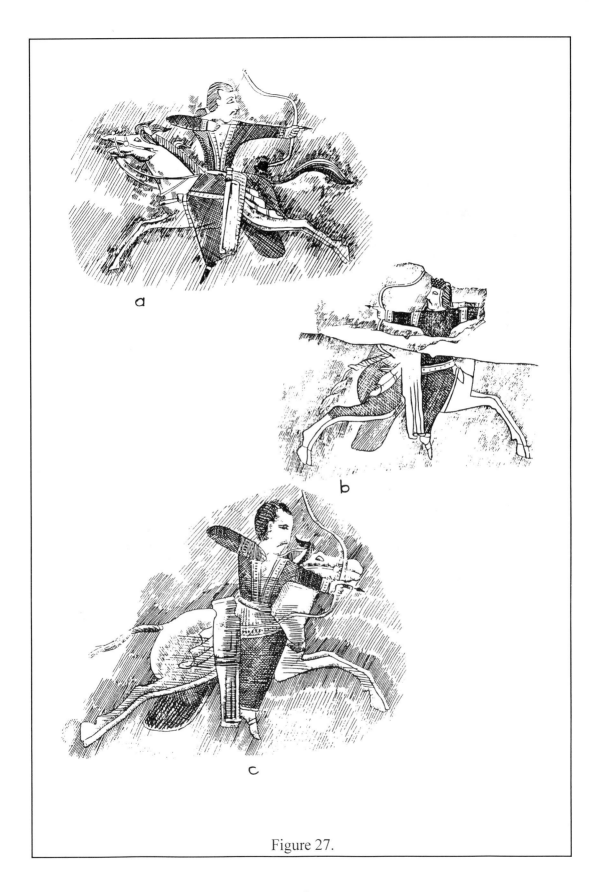

a

b

c

Figure 27.

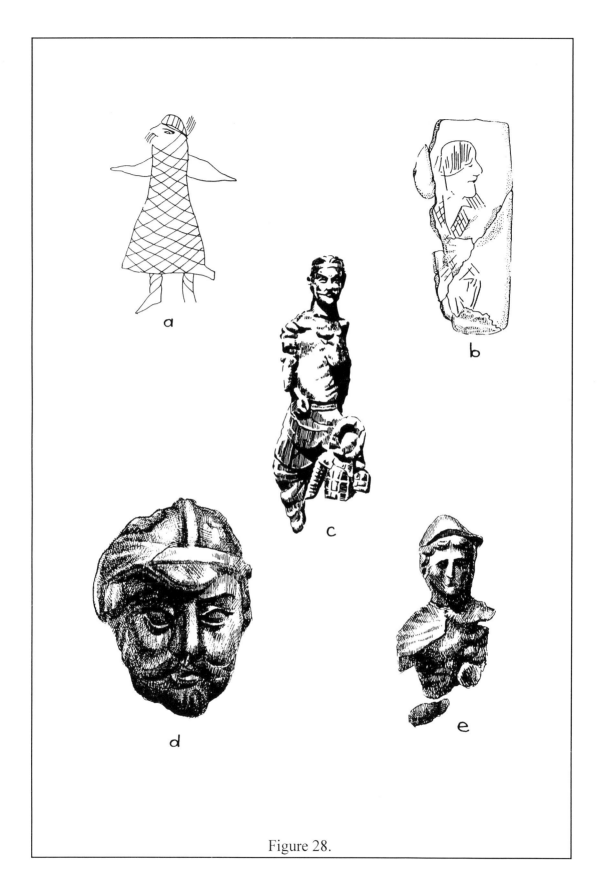

Figure 28.

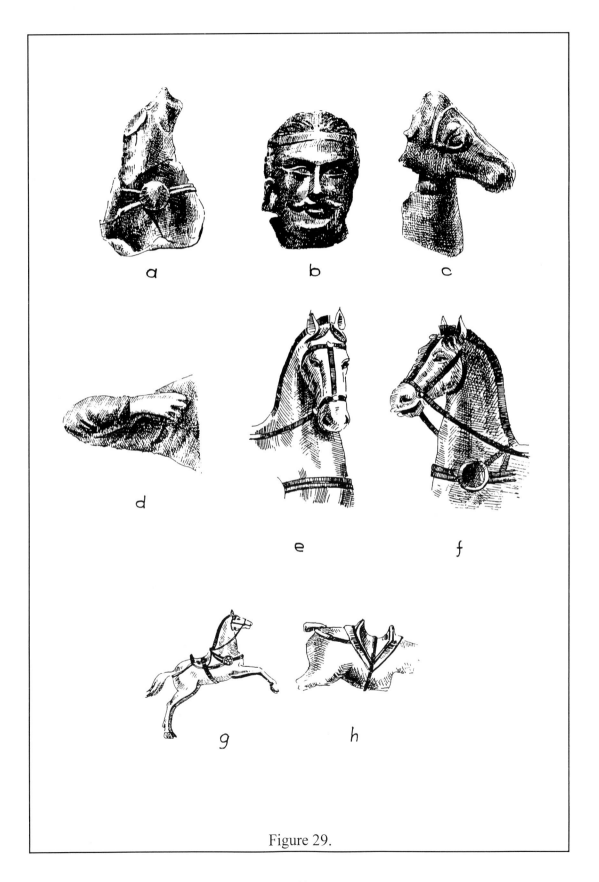

Figure 29.

Figure 30.

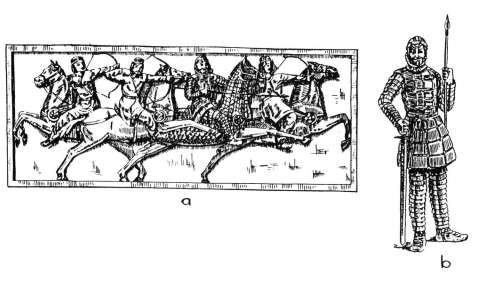

a

b

c

d

Figure 31.

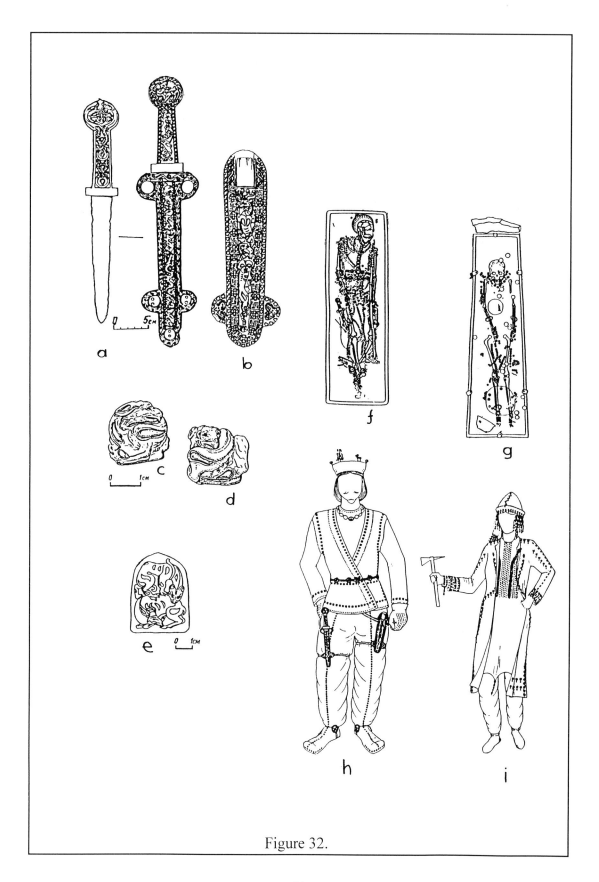

Figure 32.

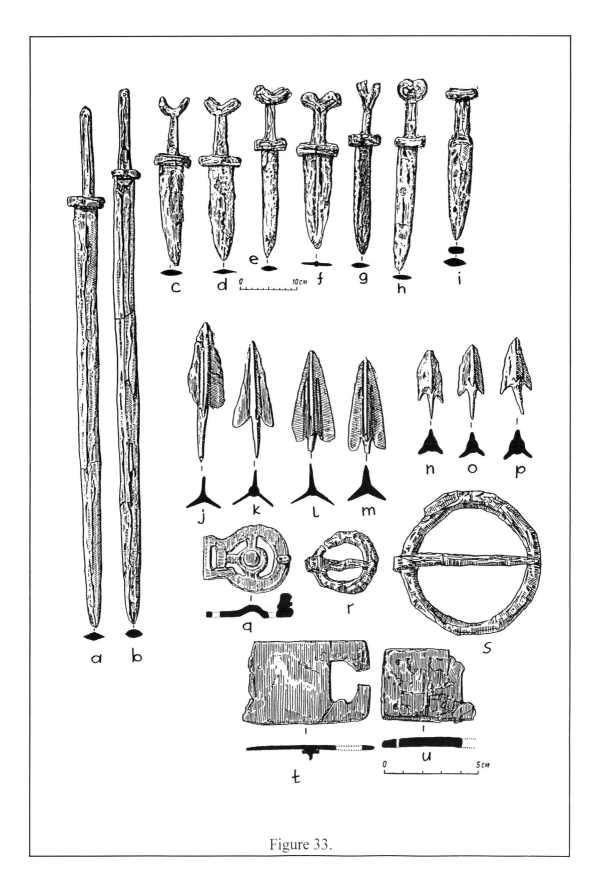

Figure 33.

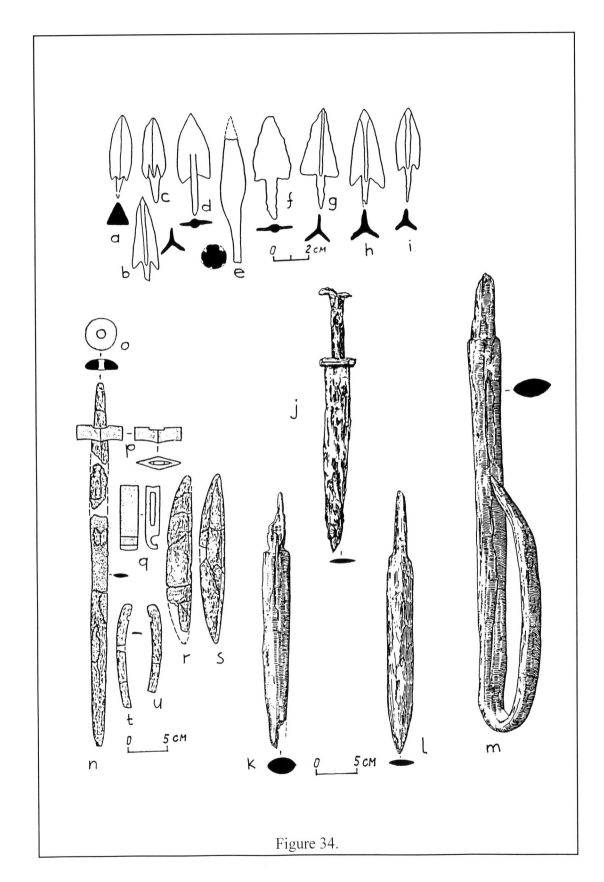

Figure 34.

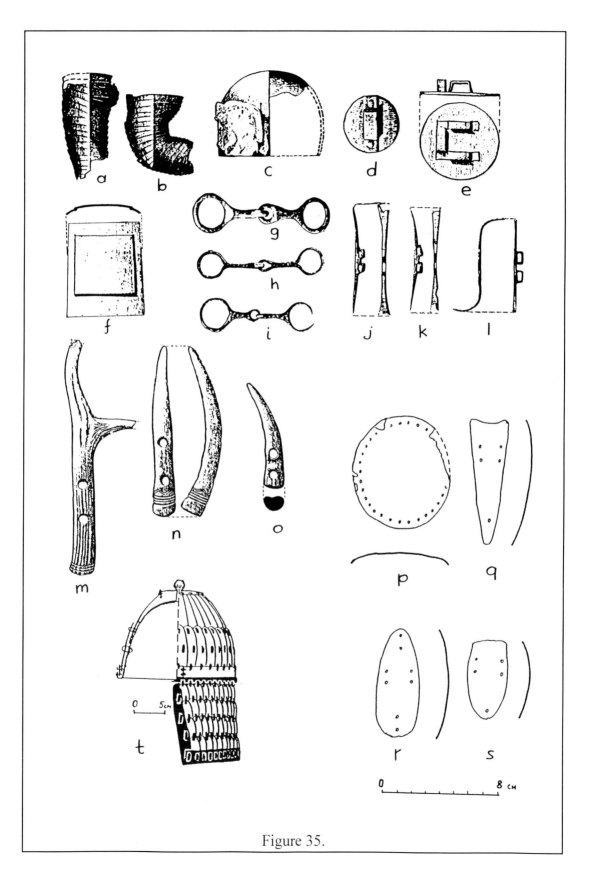

Figure 35.

67

Figure 36.

Figure 37.

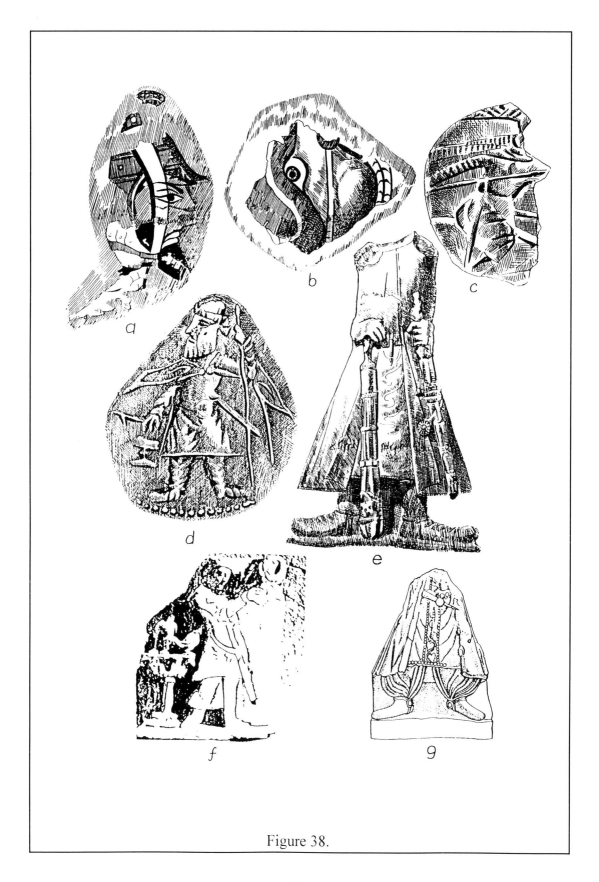

Figure 38.

Figure 39.

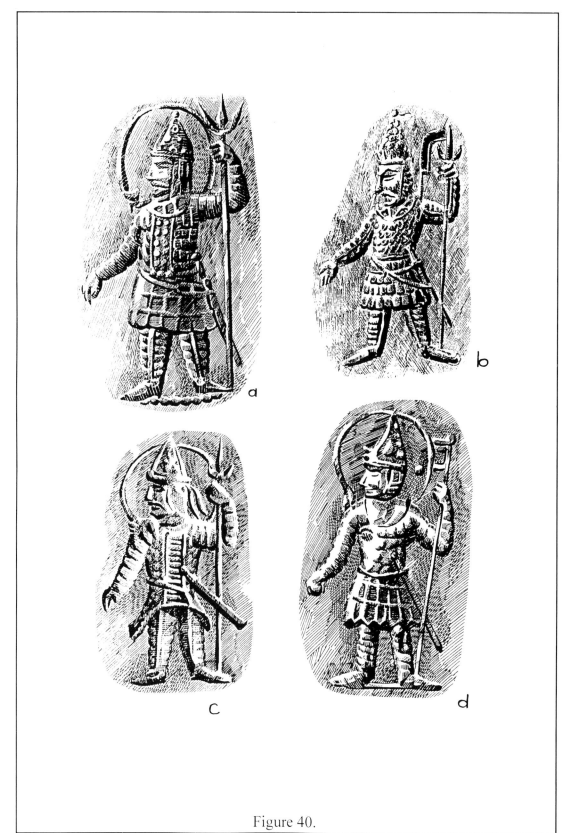

Figure 40.

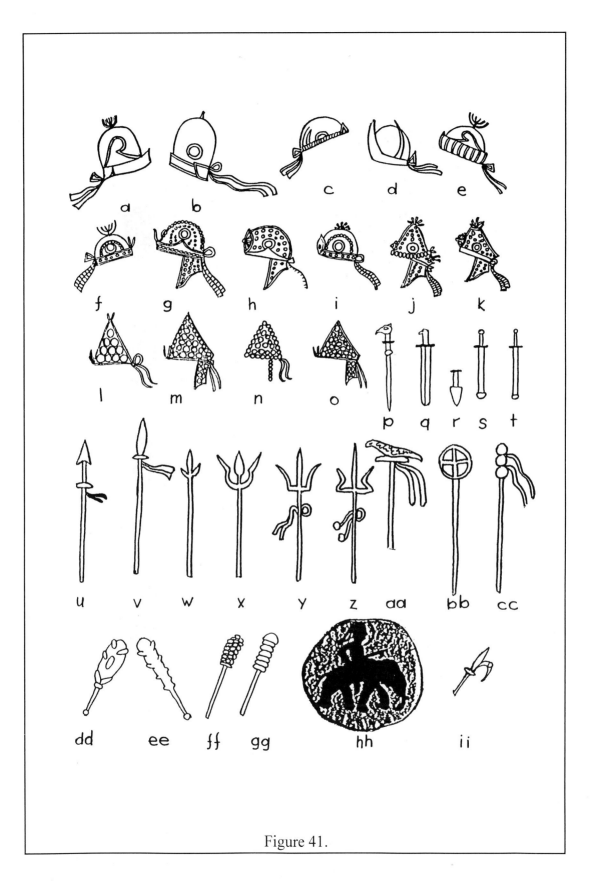

Figure 41.

Figure 42.

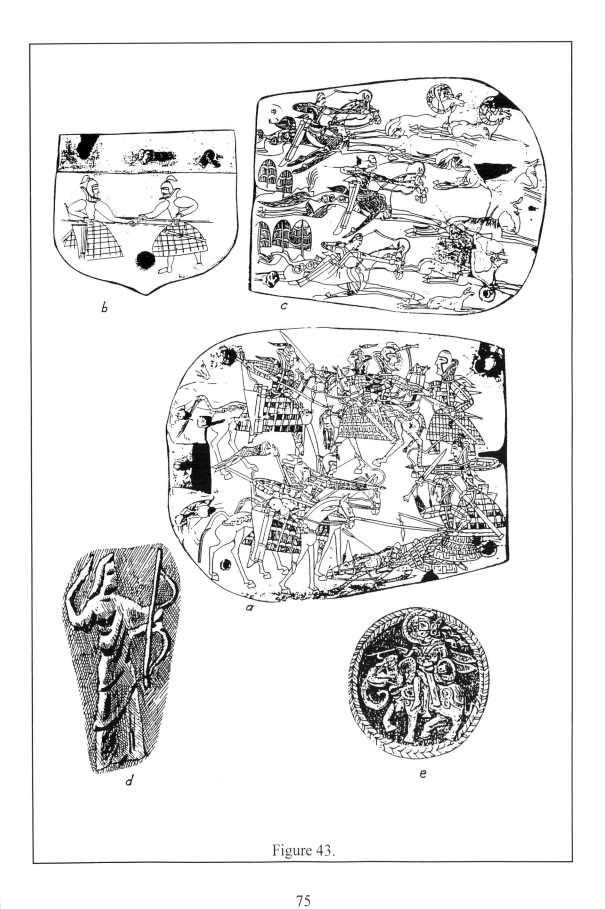

Figure 43.

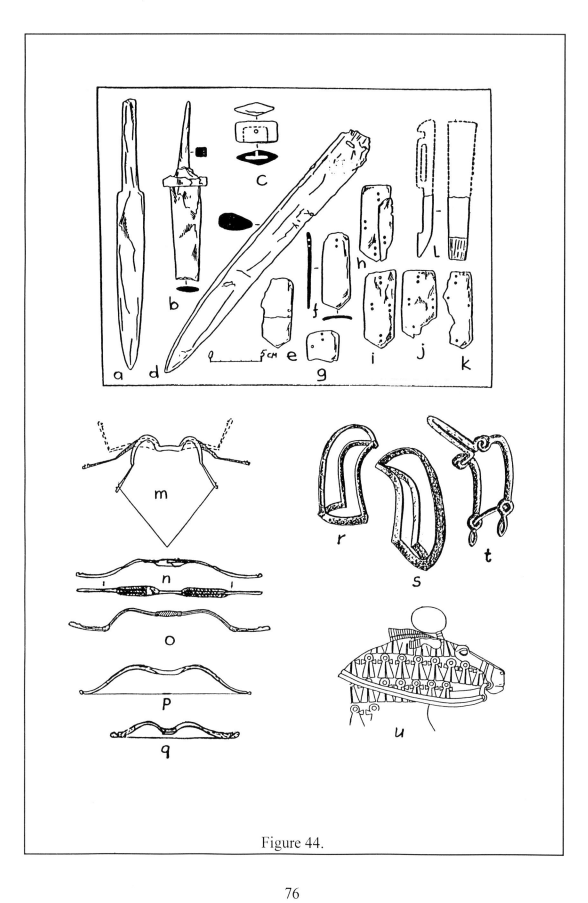

Figure 44.

Figure 45.

Figure 46.

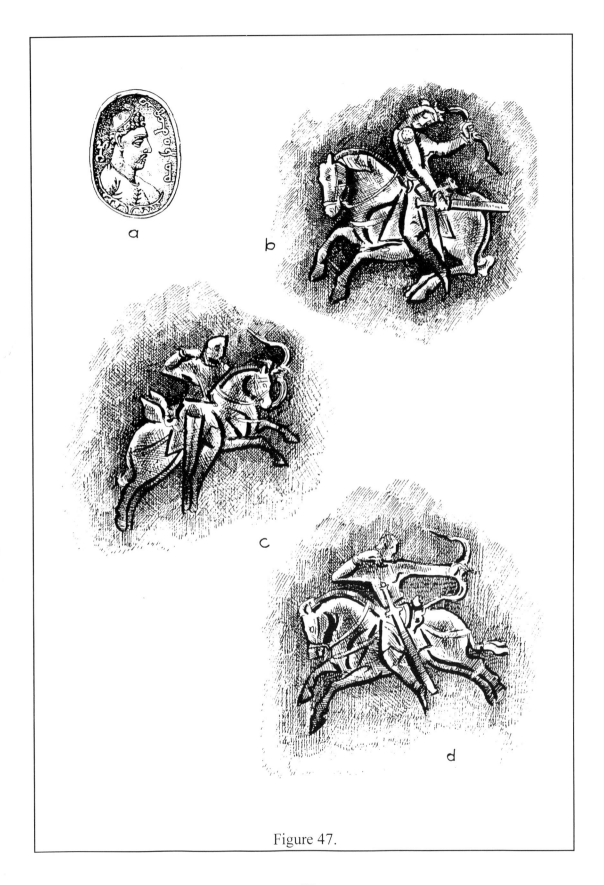

Figure 47.